Revelation

THE CROSSWAY CLASSIC COMMENTARIES

Revelation

by

Matthew Henry

Series Editors

Alister McGrath and J. I. Packer

CROSSWAY BOOKS

A DIVISION OF GOOD NEWS PUBLISHERS

WHEATON, ILLINOIS • NOTTINGHAM, ENGLAND

Revelation

Published by Crossway Books
    A division of Good News Publishers
    1300 Crescent Street
    Wheaton, Illinois 60187

First printing, 1999

Printed in the United States of America

Library of Congress Cataloging-in-Publication Data
Henry, Matthew, 1662–1714.
    Revelation / by Matthew Henry.
        p.   cm. — (The Crossway classic commentaries)
    ISBN 1-58134-065-6 (pbk. : alk. paper)
    1. Bible. N.T. Revelation—Commentaries. I. Title. II. Series.
BS2825.3.H395 1999
228'.077—dc21   99-11106
                                       CIP

15	14	13	12	11	10	09	08	07	06	05	04	03	02	01	00	99
15	14	13	12	11	10	9	8	7	6	5	4	3	2	1		

First British edition 1999

Production and Printing in the United States of America for
CROSSWAY BOOKS
Norton Street, Nottingham, England NG7 3HR

ISBN 1-85684-187-1

Contents

Series Preface

The purpose of the Crossway Classic Commentaries is to make some of the most valuable commentaries on the books of the Bible, by some of the greatest Bible teachers and theologians in the last 500 years, available to a new generation. These books will help today's readers learn truth, wisdom, and devotion from such authors as J. C. Ryle, Martin Luther, John Calvin, J. B. Lightfoot, John Owen, Charles Spurgeon, Charles Hodge, and Matthew Henry.

We do not apologize for the age of some of the items chosen. In the realm of practical exposition promoting godliness, the old is often better than the new. Spiritual vision and authority, based on an accurate handling of the biblical text, are the qualities that have been primarily sought in deciding what to include.

So far as is possible, everything is tailored to the needs and enrichment of thoughtful readers—lay Christians, students, and those in the ministry. The originals, some of which were written at a high technical level, have been abridged as needed, simplified stylistically, and unburdened of foreign words. However, the intention of this series is never to change any thoughts of the original authors, but to faithfully convey them in an understandable fashion.

The publishers are grateful to Dr. Alister McGrath of Wycliffe Hall, Oxford, Dr. J. I. Packer of Regent College, Vancouver, and Watermark of Norfolk, England, for the work of selecting and editing that now brings this project to fruition.

THE PUBLISHERS
Crossway Books
Wheaton, Illinois

Introduction

The *Exposition of the Old and New Testaments* by Matthew Henry (1662-1714) was the first work of its kind, and still stands as the greatest. Notes ("annotations") on the hard places in the Bible had been published before, notably by the Puritan Matthew Poole, but Henry goes through every verse of the Bible, explaining, analyzing, and applying in a way that is at once simple, spiritual, sober, sensible, stimulating, and searching. Thoroughly scholarly in its unobtrusive way, and embodying the best wisdom of a century and a half of Bible commentary work by Calvin and his fellow Reformers and by Puritans in England and Scotland, Henry's exposition was hailed as having classic status from the moment it began to appear.

George Whitefield, God's lightning rod of revival on both sides of the Atlantic in the mid-eighteenth century, used to travel with his Bible, his Anglican Prayer Book, and the six volumes of Matthew Henry as his resources for ministry. He read Henry from cover to cover four times, mostly on his knees, and many of his sermons were little more than echoes of Henry (and none the worse, said his discerning hearers, for that).

Forty years ago I produced a commentary list for ministerial students in which I exhorted them to sell their shirts to buy Matthew Henry. Some, I find, still recall my advice, and I am glad, for I thought it was good advice then, and I think it is good advice now. It would be almost scandalous if in this Classic Commentaries series Matthew Henry did not make an appearance (*3 John* in the volume on 1, 2, and 3 John and now *Revelation*).

Henry's biblical exposition was actually a write-up of material that he deployed from his pulpit each Sunday morning and afternoon for an hour at a time (which explains why his services lasted three hours, for he preached a sermon as well). Reading and commenting on a chapter of the Bible was for Henry a part of public worship in its own right. Henry himself died after preparing for the press his fifth volume, which goes to the end of Acts; but preacher friends, drawing on his notes, finished the work, and it was William Tong, who preached at Henry's funeral and wrote of his life, who completed his account of the book of Revelation.

Christian study of Revelation often assumes that since the book calls itself a "prophecy" (Rev. 1:3; 22:19), its main purpose must be to predict, through its code of symbols; chapters 4—22 must therefore be the ones that really matter, and Christ's letters to the seven churches are just a preface and a warmup. Interpreters debate whether the symbolic dramas of 4—22 all belong to John's lifetime (the preterist view), or are still to come (the futurist view), or cover all Christian history from Christ's first coming to his return (the historicist view), or picture generically the recurring dynamics of the ongoing war between Christ's kingdom and Satan's (the parallelist view, so called because parallel visions of the war between Christ's two comings are evidently there, and also because John just as evidently sets the glories of Christ's kingdom in parallel to their demonic counterparts in the persecuting Roman Empire).

If, of course, we see Christ's letters as the real heart and burden of the book, and the rest as a long visionary appendix in which Christ confirms his promise to overcomers by celebrating his own past and future overcomings of Satan, some form of the fourth view will seem self-evident. But be that as it may, Henry's concern is not to help us choose between these alternatives. Sidestepping all speculation about the precise references of the symbols in what Michael Wilcock calls this "gorgeous picture-book," he concentrates on direct pastoral and devotional application of the text as it comes. This makes his exposition a refreshment to me, and I hope it will refresh you too.

J. I. PACKER

Introduction to the Revelation of St. John the Divine

It ought to be no prejudice to the credit and authority of this book that it has been rejected by men of corrupt minds, such as Cerdon and Marcion, and doubted by men of better character; for that has been the lot of other parts of holy writ, and of the divine Author of Scripture himself. The image and superscription of this book are truly sacred and divine, and the matter of it agreeable with other prophetic books, particularly Ezekiel and Daniel. The church of God has generally received it and found good counsel and a great comfort in it.

From the beginning the church of God has been blessed with prophecy. That glorious prediction of breaking the serpent's head was the stay and support of the age of the patriarchs; and the many prophecies concerning the Messiah to come were the Gospel of the Old Testament. Christ himself prophesied about the destruction of Jerusalem. At about the time this was fulfilled, Christ instructed the apostle John to write this book of Revelation and to deliver it to the church as a prediction of the most important events that would happen to it, to the end of time, for the support of the faith of his people and the direction of their hope. It is called the Revelation because in it God discloses those things that could never have been discovered by the reasonings of the human mind—those deep things of God that no one knows except for the Spirit of God and those to whom he reveals them.

Revelation
Chapter 1

Introduction

This chapter is a general preface to the whole book and contains:

1. An inscription, declaring its origin and purpose (verses 1-2).
2. The apostolic blessing pronounced on all who take due notice of the contents of this book (verses 3-8).
3. A glorious vision or appearance of the Lord Jesus Christ to the apostle John when he gave him this revelation (verses 9-20).

Verses 1-2

The revelation of Jesus Christ, which God gave him to show his servants what must soon take place. He made it known by sending his angel to his servant John, who testifies to everything he saw—that is, the word of God and the testimony of Jesus Christ.

Here we have:

1. What we may call the pedigree of this book.

a. It is **the revelation of Jesus Christ.** This is true of the whole Bible, for all **revelation** comes through Christ, and all **revelation** centers on him; especially "in these last days he has spoken to us by his Son" (Hebrews 1:2) and about his Son. Christ, as the King of his church, has been pleased so far to let his church know by what rules and methods he will proceed in his government; and as the Prophet of the church, he has made known to us the things that will take place later on.

b. It is a **revelation ... which God gave him.** Though Christ is himself God and as such has light and life in himself, yet, as he sustains the office of "mediator between God and men" (1 Timothy 2:5), he receives his instructions from the Father. The human nature of Christ, though endowed with the greatest wisdom, judgment, and discernment, could not through the process of reason discover these great events, which, not being produced by natural causes, could be the object only of divine prescience and must come to a created mind only by **revelation.** Our Lord Jesus is the great Trustee of divine **revelation**; it is to him that we owe the knowledge we have of what we are to expect from God and what he expects from us.

c. This revelation Christ **made . . . known by sending his angel.** Notice here the wonderful order of divine revelation. God gave it to Christ, and Christ used an angel to communicate it to the churches. The angels are God's messengers; they are ministering spirits to the heirs of salvation; they are Christ's servants; principalities and powers are subject to them; all the angels of God are obliged to worship him.

d. The angels were sent **to his servant John.** As the angels are messengers of Christ, the ministers are the messengers of the churches. What they receive from heaven, they are to communicate to the churches. John was the apostle chosen for this service. Some think he was the only apostle surviving at that time, the rest having sealed their testimony with their blood. This was to be the last book of divine revelation and was therefore given to the church by the last of the apostles. John was the beloved disciple. He was, under the new testament, like the prophet Daniel under the old—"highly esteemed" (Daniel 9:23); he was Christ's servant; he was an apostle, an evangelist, and a prophet; he served Christ in all three extraordinary offices of the church. James was an apostle, but not a prophet or evangelist. Matthew was an apostle and evangelist, but not a prophet. Luke was an evangelist, but neither a prophet nor apostle. John was all three. So Christ calls him in an eminent sense **his servant John.**

John had to deliver this message to the church, to all Christ's servants, for the revelation was not just meant for Christ's special servants, his ministers, but for *all* his servants, the members of the church. They all have a right to the messages of God, and all have a concerned interest in them.

2. Here we have the subject matter of this revelation, namely, the things that **must soon take place.** The evangelists give an account of the things that have happened; prophecy gives us an account of things to come. These future events are shown, not in the clearest light in which God could have set them, but in such a light as he saw most fit and that would best serve his wise and holy purposes. Had they been as clearly foretold in all their circumstances as God could have revealed them, the prediction might have prevented their being accomplished. But they were foretold more darkly, to instill in us a deep respect for the Scriptures, and to engage our attention and excite our inquiry. We have in this revelation a general idea about the methods of divine providence and government in and about the church, and many good lessons can be learned here. These events, it is said, were such as must definitely take place, and **must soon take place.**

That is, they would begin to take place very soon, and they would all take place in a short time, for now the last ages of the world had arrived.

3. Here is an attestation of the prophecy (verse 2). It was shown to John, who testifies to **the word of God** and to **the testimony of Jesus Christ** and of **everything he saw.** It can be observed that the historical books of the Old Testament do not always have the name of their writers attached to them (e.g., the books of Judges, 1 and 2 Kings, and 1 and 2 Chronicles). But the prophetic books always have the name of the prophets attached to them (e.g., the books of Isaiah, Jeremiah, etc.). It is the same in the New Testament. John does not have his name written in his first letter, but he does in this prophecy, so that he is prepared to vouch for it and stand up for its truth. He does not just give his name, but he adds his office. He witnessed to the Word of God in general and bore witness to Jesus in particular, and to everything that he saw. He was an eyewitness and did not conceal anything he saw. Nothing recorded in this vision was his own invention or from his own imagination. It was all **the word of God** and the **testimony of Jesus Christ.** He neither added anything to it, nor kept back any part of God's counsels.

Verses 3-8

Blessed is the one who reads the words of this prophecy, and blessed are those who hear it and take to heart what is written in it, because the time is near.

John,

To the seven churches in the province of Asia:

Grace and peace to you from him who is, and who was, and who is to come, and from the seven spirits before his throne, and from Jesus Christ, who is the faithful witness, the firstborn from the dead, and the ruler of the kings of the earth.

To him who loves us and has freed us from our sins by his blood, and has made us to be a kingdom and priests to serve his God and Father—to him be glory and power for ever and ever! Amen.

Look, he is coming with the clouds,

and every eye will see him,

even those who pierced him;

and all the peoples of the earth will mourn because of him.

So shall it be! Amen.

"I am the Alpha and the Omega," says the Lord God, "who is, and who was, and who is to come, the Almighty."

We have here an apostolic blessing on those who give due respect to this divine revelation. This blessing is given both in a general way and in a specific way.

1. The general way this blessing is given refers to all who either read or

hear the words of the prophecy. This blessing seems to be pronounced with the purpose of encouraging us to study this book, and not to become tired of looking into it just because it contains many things that are obscure. It will repay the effort of the careful and attentive reader. Notice:

a. It is a blessed privilege to enjoy the words of God. This was one of the principal advantages the Jews had over the Gentiles.

b. It is a blessed thing to study the Scriptures. Those who search the Scriptures are spending their time well.

c. It is a privilege not only to read the Scriptures ourselves, but to hear them read by others who are qualified to give us their meaning and to help us understand them.

d. We are not blessed if we just read and hear the Scriptures; we must **take to heart** (verse 3) what is written in them. We must keep them in our memories, in our minds, in our affections, and in our practice; then we will be blessed indeed.

e. The nearer we come to doing what the Scriptures say, the more we will study them. **The time is near** (verse 3), and we should be even more attentive to the Scriptures as we see the day of our Lord approaching.

2. The apostolic blessing is pronounced especially and particularly **to the seven churches in the province of Asia** (verse 4). These seven churches are named in verse 11: "Ephesus, Smyrna, Pergamum, Thyatira, Sardis, Philadelphia and Laodicea." Specific messages are sent to each of them, as is recorded in chapters 2—3. The apostle's blessing is more specifically directed to these churches as they were nearest to him, since he was now on the island of Patmos. He may have been looking after them, with some of the other apostles if any of them were still alive. We observe here:

a. What the blessing is that he pronounces on all the faithful in these churches—**grace and peace** (verse 4), holiness and comfort. **Grace** is God's goodwill toward us and his good work in us. **Peace** is the sweet evidence and assurance of this grace. There can be no true peace when there is no true grace; and where grace is, peace will follow.

b. Note where this blessing comes from. In whose name does the apostle bless the churches? In the name of God and of the whole Trinity. For this is an act of adoration, and God only is the proper object of it. His ministers must bless the people in God's name, and only in his name.

(1) The Father is named first. God the Father may be taken either essentially, for God as God, or personally, for the first Person in the ever blessed Trinity, the God and Father of our Lord Jesus Christ. He is described as the Jehovah **who is, and who was, and who is to come** (verse 4). He is eternal, unchanging, the same to the Old Testament church that was and to the New Testament church that is, and he will be the same to the church triumphant that is to come.

(2) The Holy Spirit is called the **seven spirits** (verse 4). This does not mean seven in number or in nature, but indicates the infinite, perfect Spirit

of God, in whom there is a diversity of gifts and workings. He is **before his throne**, for as God made, so he governs all things by his Spirit.

(3) The Lord Jesus Christ. John mentions him after the Spirit because he intended to expand upon the person of Christ as God revealed in the flesh, whom he had seen living on earth before, and now saw again in a glorious form.

5. Notice the special account we have here of Christ. **And from Jesus Christ, who is the faithful witness, the firstborn from the dead, and the ruler of the kings of the earth. To him who loves us and has freed us from our sins by his blood . . .**

First, he is **the faithful witness.** He was from eternity a witness to all the counsels of God. "No one has ever seen God, but God the only Son, who is at the Father's side, has made him known" (John 1:18). He was in time a faithful witness to the revealed will of God, who "in these last days . . . has spoken to us by his Son" (Hebrews 1:2). We may safely rely on his testimony, for he is **the faithful witness.** He cannot be deceived and cannot deceive us.

Second, he is **the firstborn from the dead,** or the first Parent and Head of the resurrection, the only one who raised himself by his own power and who will by the same power raise up his people from their graves to everlasting honor. He has given birth to them a second time unto a living hope through his resurrection from the dead.

Third, he is **the ruler of the kings of the earth.** Earthly kings derive their authority from Christ, and through him their power is limited and their anger restrained. Through Christ their counsels are overruled, and they are accountable to him. This is the good news brought to the church, and it is clear evidence of the Godhead of Christ, who is "Lord of lords and King of kings" (Revelation 17:14).

Fourth, he is the great friend of his church and people. He has done great things for them, out of pure affection. He has loved them, and, pursuing this everlasting love, he has **freed us from our sins by his blood.** Sin leaves a stain upon the soul, a stain of guilt and pollution. Only Christ's blood can remove this stain. Christ was willing to shed his own blood to purchase pardon and purity for us.

Christ has also **made us to be a kingdom and priests to serve his God and Father** (verse 6). Having justified and sanctified us, he makes us kings to serve his Father—that is, in his Father's account, with his approbation, and for his glory. As kings, his people overcome the world, mortify sin, govern their own spirits, conquer Satan, have power and prevalence with God in prayer, and will judge the world. He has made them **priests** and has given them access to God, enabling them to enter into the holiest place and offer spiritual and acceptable sacrifices. He has anointed them for this work, and because of these high honors and favors, they are bound to give him dominion and glory forever.

Fifth, Christ will judge the world. **Look, he is coming with the clouds, and every eye will see him** (verse 7). This book, Revelation, begins and ends with the prediction of the second coming of the Lord Jesus Christ. We should set ourselves to meditate frequently on the second coming of Christ and keep it in the eye of our faith and expectation. John speaks as if he saw that day: **Look, he is coming,** as definitely as if he saw Christ with his own eyes. **He is coming with the clouds,** like a chariot. Christ's appearance will be public: **every eye will see him.** The eye of his people, the eye of his enemies, every eye, yours and mine, will see Christ.

Even those who pierced him. His coming will bring terror to those who pierced him and have not repented, and to all who have wounded and crucified him afresh by their apostasy of him. "It is impossible for those who have once been enlightened, who have tasted the heavenly gift, who have shared in the Holy Spirit, who have tasted the goodness of the word of God and the powers of the coming age, if they fall away, to be brought back to repentance, because to their loss they are crucifying the Son of God all over again and subjecting him to public disgrace" (Hebrews 6:4-6). **All the peoples of the earth will mourn because of him.** Christ will come, to the astonishment of the pagan world, for Christ comes to take vengeance on those who do not know God as well as on those who do not obey the Gospel of Christ.

Sixth, this account of Christ is ratified and confirmed by himself. **"I am the Alpha and the Omega," says the Lord God, "who is, and who was, and who is to come, the Almighty."** Here our Lord Jesus justly claims the same honor and power that is ascribed to the Father in verse 4. **"I am the Alpha and the Omega."** Christ is the beginning and the end. All things are from him and for him. He is **the Almighty**; he is the eternal and unchanged One. Surely, whoever presumes to blot out one character of this name of Christ deserves his name blotted out of the book of life. Those who honor Christ, Christ will honor; but those who despise him will be lightly esteemed.

Verses 9-20

I, John, your brother and companion in the suffering and kingdom and patient endurance that are ours in Jesus, was on the island of Patmos because of the word of God and the testimony of Jesus. On the Lord's Day I was in the Spirit, and I heard behind me a loud voice like a trumpet, which said: "Write on a scroll what you see and send it to the seven churches: to Ephesus, Smyrna, Pergamum, Thyatira, Sardis, Philadelphia and Laodicea."

I turned around to see the voice that was speaking to me. And when I turned I saw seven golden lampstands, and among the lampstands was someone "like a son of man," dressed in a robe reaching down to

his feet and with a golden sash around his chest. His h .ad and hair were white like wool, as white as snow, and his eyes were like blazing fire. His feet were like bronze glowing in a furnace, and his voice was like the sound of rushing waters. In his right hand he held seven stars, and out of his mouth came a sharp double-edged sword. His face was like the sun shining in all its brilliance.

When I saw him, I fell at his feet as though dead. Then he placed his right hand on me and said: "Do not be afraid. I am the First and the Last. I am the Living One; I was dead, and behold I am alive for ever and ever! And I hold the keys of death and Hades.

"Write, therefore, what you have seen, what is now and what will take place later. The mystery of the seven stars that you saw in my right hand and of the seven golden lampstands is this: The seven stars are the angels of the seven churches, and the seven lampstands are the seven churches."

We now come to that glorious vision that the apostle had of the Lord Jesus Christ when Christ came to deliver this revelation to him. We observe:

1. The account given of the person who was favored with this vision. He describes himself:

a. By his present state and condition. **I, John, your brother and companion in the suffering and kingdom and patient endurance that are ours in Jesus, was on the island of Patmos because of the word of God and the testimony of Jesus** (verse 9). He was **your brother and companion in the suffering and kingdom and patient endurance that are ours in Jesus.** He was at this time, as the rest of the true Christians were, a persecuted man, banished, and perhaps imprisoned for his adherence to Christ. He was their **brother**, though an apostle. He seems to value his relationship to the church more than his authority in it. Judas was one of the Twelve, but not a brother in the family of God. God's children should seek fellowship and companionship with each other, and John was their **companion in . . . suffering.** God's persecuted servants do not suffer alone. Similar trials befall other people.

John was their companion in **patient endurance**, being not only a sharer with them in suffering circumstances, but in suffering graces. If we have the patience of the saints, we should not complain when we meet with their trials. John was their **brother and companion in the suffering and kingdom and patient endurance that are ours in Jesus.** John was a sufferer for Christ's cause, for asserting Christ's kingly power over the church in the world, and for adhering to it against all who would usurp it. In this account John gives details about his present state, acknowledges that he sympathizes with other believers, endeavors to give them counsel and comfort, and encourages their more careful attention to what he had to say to them from Christ, their common Lord.

b. By the place where he was when he was favored with this vision. He was **on the island of Patmos** (verse 9). John does not say who banished him there. It becomes Christians to speak sparingly and modestly about their own sufferings. Patmos is an island in the Aegean Sea, one of the Cyclades, and was about thirty-five miles in width. But under this confinement it was the apostle's comfort that he did not suffer as an evildoer but because of **the testimony of Jesus**, for bearing witness to Christ as Immanuel, the Saviour. "'The virgin will be with child and will give birth to a son, and they will call him Immanuel'—which means, 'God with us'" (Matthew 1:23). This was a cause worth suffering for, and the Spirit of glory and of God rested on this persecuted apostle.

c. The day and time in which he had this vision. It was **on the Lord's Day** (verse 10). This was the day that Christ had separated and set apart for himself, just as the Eucharist is called the Lord's Supper. Surely this can be no other than the Christian sabbath—the first day of the week, to be observed in remembrance of the resurrection of Christ. Let us who call him our Lord honor him on his own day, the day the Lord made, in which we should rejoice.

d. The frame that his soul was in at this time. **I was in the Spirit** (verse 10). He was not only in rapture when he received the vision, but *before* he received it. He was in a serious, heavenly, spiritual frame of mind and soul, under the blessed, gracious influences of the Spirit of God. God usually prepares the souls of his people for uncommon manifestations of himself by the quickening, sanctifying influences of his good Spirit. Those who want to enjoy fellowship with God **on the Lord's Day** must endeavor to remove their thoughts and affections from the flesh and fleshly things and be wholly taken up with things of a spiritual nature.

2. The apostle gives an account of what he heard when he was **in the Spirit** (verse 10). **I heard behind me a loud voice like a trumpet, which said: "Write on a scroll what you see and send it to the seven churches"** (verse 10). An alarm was given as with the sound of **a trumpet**; he heard a **loud voice,** the voice of Christ applying to himself the character mentioned before, "the Alpha and the Omega" (verse 8) and commanding the apostle to write down the things that were now revealed to him, and to send it immediately **to the seven churches** of Asia: **to Ephesus, Smyrna, Pergamum, Thyatira, Sardis, Philadelphia and Laodicea** (verse 11). Thus our Lord Jesus Christ, the Captain of our salvation, gave the apostle notice of his glorious appearance, as with the sound of **a trumpet.**

3. We now have an account of what he saw. **I turned around to see the voice that was speaking to me. And when I turned I saw seven golden lampstands** (verse 12). He **turned around to see the voice,** whose it was and where it came from, and then a wonderful vision opened itself to him.

a. He saw a representation of the church under the emblem of **seven golden lampstands.** These **lampstands** are explained in verse 20: **The mystery of the . . . seven golden lampstands is this: . . . the seven lampstands are the seven churches.** The **churches** are compared to **lampstands** because they uphold the light of the Gospel so effectively. The **churches** are not the candles—Christ alone is our Light, and his Gospel our lamp; but they receive their light from Christ and the Gospel and hold it up so others can see it. They are **golden lampstands,** for they should be precious and pure, like fine gold; not only the ministers, but the members of the churches should be like this. Their light should shine before men, so that other people will give glory to God. "Let your light shine before men, that they may see your good deeds and praise your Father in heaven" (Matthew 5:16).

b. He saw a representation of the Lord Jesus Christ in the middle of the golden lampstands: . . . someone **"like a son of man," dressed in a robe reaching down to his feet and with a golden sash around his chest. His head and hair were white like wool, as white as snow, and his eyes were like blazing fire. His feet were like bronze glowing in a furnace, and his voice was like the sound of rushing waters. In his right hand he held seven stars, and out of his mouth came a sharp double-edged sword. His face was like the sun shining in all its brilliance** (verses 13-16). Christ had promised to be with his churches always, to the end of the world ("Surely I will be with you always, to the very end of the age," Matthew 28:20), filling them with light and life and love, for he brings the church to life as he is the Soul of the church. Here we may observe:

(1) The glorious form in which Christ appeared, in several particulars.

First, he was **dressed in a robe reaching down to his feet** (verse 13). This was a princely and priestly robe, denoting righteousness and honor.

Second, he was **dressed . . . with a golden sash around his chest** (verse 13). The high priest's breastplate, on which the names of Christ's people were engraved, was already being worn, in readiness to do all the work of a Redeemer.

Third, **his head and hair were white like wool, as white as snow** (verse 14). He was the Ancient of Days: "thrones were set in place, and the Ancient of Days took his seat. His clothing was as white as snow; the hair of his head was white like wool" (Daniel 7:9). His white hair was not an indication of decay, but a crown of glory.

Fourth, **his eyes were like blazing fire** (verse 14), piercing the hearts and consciences of men, scattering terror among his adversaries.

Fifth, **his feet were like bronze glowing in a furnace** (verse 15). His feet were strong and steadfast, supporting his own interests, subduing his enemies and grinding them to powder.

Sixth, **his voice was like the sound of rushing waters** (verse 15). His voice was like many rivers converging. He can and will make himself heard to those who are far away as well as to those who are nearby. His Gospel is a mighty stream fed by the highest springs of wisdom and knowledge.

Seventh, **in his right hand he held seven stars** (verse 16). The ministers of the seven churches, who are under his direction, derive all their light and influence from him and are secured and preserved by him.

Eighth, **out of his mouth came a sharp double-edged sword** (verse 16). His Word, which both wounds and heals, strikes at the sins on the right hand and on the left.

Ninth, **his face was like the sun shining in all its brilliance** (verse 16). The brightness of his shining was too strong and dazzling for mortal eyes to behold.

(2) The impression this appearance of Christ made on the apostle John. **When I saw him, I fell at his feet as though dead** (verse 17). John was overcome with the greatness and luster and glory in which Christ appeared, though he had been so well-acquainted with him before. How good it is for us that God speaks to us through men like ourselves, whose appearances do not frighten us, for no one can see God's face and live.

(3) The condescending goodness of the Lord Jesus to his disciples. **Then he placed his right hand on me and said: "Do not be afraid. I am the First and the Last. I am the Living One; I was dead, and behold I am alive for ever and ever! And I hold the keys of death and Hades"** (verses 17-18). When Christ **placed his right hand** on John, he raised him up; he did not plead against him with great power, but put strength into him and spoke kind words to him. These words gave comfort and encouragement: **"Do not be afraid."** Christ banished the slavish fears of his disciple.

These words were also words of instruction, as they told John the nature of the person who was appearing to him. Here Christ acquaints John with aspects of his being.

First, with his divine nature: **"I am the First and the Last"** (verse 17).

Second, with his previous sufferings: **"I was dead"** (verse 18)—the same suffering that Christ's apostles saw when he died on the cross for the sins of mankind.

Third, with his resurrection life: **"I am the Living One. I was dead, and behold I am alive for ever and ever!"** (verse 18). Having conquered death and opened the grave, Christ lives an everlasting life.

Fourth, with his office and authority: **"I hold the keys of death and Hades"** (verse 18). Christ rules over the invisible world, opening doors that no one can shut, and shutting doors that no one can open. He opens the gates of death as he pleases, and the gates of the eternal world, of happiness or misery, as the Judge of everyone, against whose sentence there is no appeal.

Fifth, with his will and pleasure that John would write about the things he had seen and the things that are and the things that will take place: **"Write, therefore, what you have seen, what is now and what will take place later"** (verse 19).

Sixth, with the meaning of the seven stars: **"The seven stars are the angels of the seven churches, and the seven lampstands are the seven churches"** (verse 20), to whom Christ now sends through John particular and relevant messages.

Revelation
Chapter 2

Introduction

The apostle John, having in the previous chapter written about the things he had seen, now writes about the things then present, as God had commanded him: "Write, therefore, what you have seen, what is now . . ." (1:19)—that is, the present state of the seven churches of Asia, with whom he had special acquaintance, and for whom he had a tender concern. He was directed to write to each of them according to their particular circumstances and to dedicate each letter to the angel of that church, that is, to the minister, or rather ministry, of that church, called angels because they were God's messengers to mankind.

In this chapter we have:

1. The message to Ephesus (verses 1-7).
2. The message to Smyrna (verses 8-11).
3. The message to Pergamum (verses 12-17).
4. The message to Thyatira (verses 18-29).

Verses 1-7

To the angel of the church in Ephesus write:

These are the words of him who holds the seven stars in his right hand and walks among the seven golden lampstands. I know your deeds, your hard work and your perseverance. I know that you cannot tolerate wicked men, that you have tested those who claim to be apostles but are not, and have found them false. You have persevered and have endured hardships for my name, and have not grown weary.

Yet I hold this against you: You have forsaken your first love. Remember the height from which you have fallen! Repent and do the things you did at first. If you do not repent, I will come to you and remove your lampstand from its place. But you have this in your favor: You hate the practices of the Nicolaitans, which I also hate.

He who has an ear, let him hear what the Spirit says to the churches. To him who overcomes, I will give the right to eat from the tree of life, which is in the paradise of God.

We have here:

1. The inscription, where we notice:

a. To whom the first of these letters is sent—**to the angel of the church in Ephesus** (verse 1). This famous church in Ephesus was planted by the apostle Paul (see Acts 19) and after that was watered by St. John, who lived there for quite some time. We can hardly suppose that Timothy was the angel or sole pastor and bishop of this church at this time, or that he who had such an excellent spirit and naturally cared for the good state of the souls of people should become so remiss as to deserve the rebukes given to the ministry of this church.

b. Notice who wrote this letter to the Ephesians. Here we have one of those titles given to Christ when he appeared to John, as recorded in chapter 1. "I saw seven golden lampstands, and among the lampstands was someone . . . In his right hand he held seven stars" (1:12-13, 16). This title has two parts.

(1) **Him who holds the seven stars in his right hand** (verse 1). Christ's ministers are under his special care and protection. It is to God's honor that he knows the number of the stars and calls them by their names. "Can you bind the beautiful Pleiades? Can you loose the cords of Orion?" (Job 38:31). And it is due to the Lord Jesus Christ's honor that the ministers of the Gospel, who are greater blessings to the church than the stars are to the world, are in his hand. He directs all their flights and orbits, fills them with light and power, and supports them, or they would crash to the ground like falling stars. They are instruments in his hand, and all the good they do is done through his hand being with them.

(2) He **walks among the seven golden lampstands** (verse 1). This refers to Christ's relationship to his churches, just as the stars spoke about his relationship to his ministers. Christ is present with his churches in an intimate way. He knows and observes their state; he takes pleasure in them, just as a person takes delight in walking around his garden. Although Christ is in heaven, he walks in the middle of his churches on earth, observing what is wrong with them and what they lack. It greatly encourages those who care for churches to know that the Lord Jesus has engraved them on the palms of his hands (Isaiah 49:16).

2. The contents of the letter, in which, as in most of those that follow, we have:

a. The commendation Christ gave to this church, both its ministers and members. He refers to this by declaring, **I know your deeds** (verse 2), and therefore both his commendation and his rebuke are to be carefully noted, for he does not speak from ignorance—he knows what he is talking about. The Ephesian church is commended:

(1) For their diligence to duty: **I know your deeds, your hard work** (verse 2). Dignity calls for duty. Those who are stars in Christ's hand always need to be moving about, dispensing light to everyone around them. **You have persevered and have endured hardships for my name, and have not grown weary** (verse 3). Christ keeps an account of each day's work, of each hour's work, that his servants do for him. This work is never in vain. "You know that your labor in the Lord is not in vain" (1 Corinthians 15:58).

(2) For their patient suffering: **your hard work and your perseverance** (verse 2). It is not enough just to be diligent; we must persevere and endure. "Endure hardship . . . like a good soldier of Christ Jesus" (2 Timothy 2:3). Ministers must have, and must exercise, great perseverance; no Christian should be without it. You must have perseverance to endure attacks from people and the rebukes of providence. You must wait with perseverance so that when you have done God's will, you may continue and finish the race.

(3) For their zeal against what was evil: **I know that you cannot tolerate wicked men** (verse 2). Not to be involved with or even tolerate evil fits in well with perseverance. While we must show everyone how meek we are, we must demonstrate that we actively oppose the sins of the wicked. This zeal of theirs was the more commendable as it was based on knowledge and built on previous observations of evil people. This is in contrast to: "I can testify about them that they are zealous for God, but their zeal is not based on knowledge" (Romans 10:2).

You have tested those who claim to be apostles but are not, and have found them false (verse 2). True zeal goes hand in hand with discretion. Nobody should be thrown out until they have been tried. Some people rose up in the church who pretended to be more than ordinary ministers, even claiming to be apostles. But their claims were examined and found to be vain and false. People who impartially search after truth will come to distinguish between falsehood and truth.

b. The rebuke given to this church: **Yet I hold this against you** (verse 4). People who have a great deal of good in them may also have a great deal of evil in them. Our Lord Jesus, as an impartial Master and Judge, takes notice of both good and evil. He starts by noting what is good and is most willing to mention this, but he also observes what is wrong and will faithfully reprove his followers for this. The sin of which Christ accused this church is their decline of zeal and holy love. **You have forsaken your first love** (verse 4). They have not forsaken the object of their love but have lost the fervent desire with which their love started. Notice:

(1) The first affections of people toward Christ and holiness and heaven are usually lively and warm. God remembered Israel's love when she followed him wherever he went.

(2) These lively affections cool down unless great care and diligence is taken to keep them exercised constantly.

(3) Christ is displeased and grieved with his people when he sees them grow remiss and cold toward him. Christ will one way or another make them realize that he does not accept this behavior from them.

c. The advice and counsel Christ gives them: **Remember the height from which you have fallen! Repent and do the things you did at first** (verse 5).

(1) Those who have lost their first love must remember how far they have fallen. They must compare their present state with their previous state and reflect on how much better they were than they are now. They must recall how much peace, strength, purity, and pleasure they have lost because they have forsaken their first love. They must remember how much more comfortably they used to be able to lie down and sleep at night, how much more cheerfully they could wake up in the morning, how much better they were able to bear afflictions, and how much more they were able to enjoy the favors of providence. They must remember how much easier it was for them to think about death and how much more they used to desire and hope for heaven.

(2) They must repent. They must be inwardly grieved and ashamed of their sinful decline. They must blame themselves for the state they are in, humbly confess this before God, and judge and condemn themselves for this.

(3) They must return and do the good deeds they did at first. They must, as it were, begin again, go back step by step until they arrive at the place where they took the first false step. They must endeavor to revive and recover their first zeal, tenderness, and seriousness, and must pray earnestly and watch diligently, as they did when they first started to follow God.

This good advice is urged, first, by a severe threat, should we choose to ignore the warning: **If you do not repent, I will come to you and remove your lampstand from its place** (verse 5). If the presence of Christ's grace and Spirit are slighted, we may expect to receive his displeasure. He will come by way of judgment, suddenly, on impenitent churches and sinners. He will remove them from the Christian fellowship and will take his Gospel, ministers, and ordinances away from them. And what will the churches or the angels of the churches do when the Gospel is removed?

Second, this advice is given to encourage them to act in the right way: **But you have this in your favor: You hate the practices of the Nicolaitans, which I also hate** (verse 6). "Even though you have declined in your love in doing what is good, yet you still hate what is evil, especially blatant evil." The Nicolaitans were a sect who hid behind the name of Christianity. They believed hateful doctrines, and they were guilty of hateful deeds, hateful toward Christ and toward all true Christians. It is to the credit of the Ephesian church that they were zealous in their hatred of this evil and that they abhorred these wicked teachings and practices. An indifferent spirit toward truth and error, good and evil, may be called charity or meekness, but it does not please Christ. Our Saviour adds this kind commendation to his severe threat to make the advice more effective.

3. We come now to the conclusion of the letter, where, as in the other letters, we have:

a. A call to be attentive: **He who has an ear, let him hear what the Spirit says to the churches** (verse 7). Notice:

(1) What is written in the Scriptures is spoken by the Spirit of God.

(2) What is said to one church, concerns all the churches, everywhere and in every age.

(3) We can make no better use of our faculties of hearing than listening to God's Word. We deserve to lose our hearing if we do not use it in this way. Those who do not hear God's call now will eventually wish that they had never had the ability to hear at all.

b. A promise of great mercy to those who overcome: **To him who overcomes, I will give the right to eat from the tree of life, which is in the paradise of God** (verse 7). The Christian life is war against sin, Satan, the world, and the flesh. It is not enough to just engage in this war—we must fight it to the end. We must never give in to our spiritual enemies but must fight the good fight until we achieve the victory, as all persevering Christians will do. This war concludes in a glorious triumph and reward. The reward that is promised here is **to eat from the tree of life** (verse 7). If Adam had been successful in his temptation, he would have eaten from the tree of life in the middle of paradise, and that would have been a sacramental assurance to him about his holy and happy state. All who persevere in their Christian trials and warfare will receive from Christ, as from the tree of life, perfection and assurance about holiness and happiness in God's paradise. This will not happen in the earthly paradise but in the heavenly one. "Then the angel showed me the river of the water of life, as clear as crystal, flowing from the throne of God and of the Lamb down the middle of the great street of the city. On each side of the river stood the tree of life, bearing twelve crops of fruit, yielding its fruit every month. And the leaves of the tree are for the healing of the nations" (22:1-2).

Verses 8-11

To the angel of the church in Smyrna write:

These are the words of him who is the First and the Last, who died and came to life again. I know your afflictions and your poverty—yet you are rich! I know the slander of those who say they are Jews and are not, but are a synagogue of Satan. Do not be afraid of what you are about to suffer. I tell you, the devil will put some of you in prison to test you, and you will suffer persecution for ten days. Be faithful, even to the point of death, and I will give you the crown of life.

He who has an ear, let him hear what the Spirit says to the churches. He who overcomes will not be hurt at all by the second death.

Now we move on to the second letter that was sent to the churches of Asia, where, as before, we observe:

1. The preface or inscription.

a. The superscription, telling us to whom it was specifically addressed: **To the angel of the church in Smyrna** (verse 8). Then, as now, Smyrna was well-known to merchants. It was a city of great trade and wealth, perhaps the only city out of the seven that is still known by the same name. Now, however, it is not known as a place of Christian worship, but as a place where Muslims worship.

b. The subscription contains another glorious title of our Lord Jesus: **the First and the Last, who died and came to life again** (verse 8), taken from 1:17-18.

(1) Jesus is **the First and the Last.** We have only a short time to pass through this world, but our Redeemer is **the First and the Last.** He is **the First** since through him everything was made. He was before all things with God and was God himself. He is **the Last,** for everything is made by him, and he will Judge everyone. This is surely the title of God from everlasting to everlasting, and it is the title of the One who is the unchanging Mediator between God and man. "Jesus Christ is the same yesterday and today and forever" (Hebrews 13:8). Through him the foundation of the church was laid in the time of the patriarchs. He is **the Last** because through him the capstone will be brought out and laid at the end of time.

(2) **Died and came to life again** (verse 8). He **died** for our sins. He **came to life again,** rising again for our justification, and he always lives to make intercession for us. He **died** and by dying bought salvation for us. He **came to life again,** and through his life he applies this salvation to us. And if when we were enemies, we are reconciled through his death, much more, now that we are reconciled, we will be saved through his life. We commemorate his death every sacrament-day, his resurrection and life every sabbath-day.

2. The theme of this letter to Smyrna. After the usual declaration of Christ's omniscience and the perfect knowledge he has of all the deeds of men, and especially of his churches, John especially notes:

a. The progress they'd made in their spiritual state. This comes in a brief parenthesis, but it is emphatic: **yet you are rich!** (verse 9). They were poor in worldly goods but rich in spiritual blessings. They were poor in spirit but rich in grace. Their spiritual riches were set off by their outward poverty. Many who are rich in worldly goods are spiritual paupers. This was the case with the church of Laodicea. But in Smyrna some who were outwardly poor were inwardly rich. They were rich in good deeds, rich in spiritual privileges, and rich in hope. Spiritual riches are usually the reward of great diligence; the diligent hand makes rich. Where there are spiritual riches, outward poverty may be borne more easily. When God's people are impoverished in this life, for the sake of Christ and a good conscience, everything is made up to them in spiritual riches, which satisfy and endure more than anything else.

b. Their sufferings. **I know your afflictions and your poverty** (verse 9). They were persecuted and even lost their possessions in the process. Those who are faithful to Christ must expect to go through many tribulations, but Jesus Christ takes particular notice of all their troubles. In all their afflictions Christ is afflicted, and he will recompense tribulation to their persecutors; and those who are persecuted, he gives rest with himself.

c. Christ knows the wickedness and the falsehood of their enemies. **I know the slander of those who say they are Jews and are not** (verse 9).

(1) That is, he knows about those who pretend to be the only special covenant people of God, as the Jews boasted even after God had rejected them.

(2) Or this refers to those who would be setting up the Jewish rites and ceremonies, which were now not only antiquated but abrogated. These people may say they only are the church of God in the world but are in fact **a synagogue of Satan.**

Observe, first, as Christ has a church in the world, the spiritual Israel of God, so the devil has his **synagogue**, his assemblies that oppose the truths of the Gospel and promote and propagate damnable errors. Such people oppose the purity and spirituality of gospel worship and promote and propagate the vain inventions of men and rites and ceremonies that never entered God's thoughts. Such assemblies are set up to revile and persecute the true worship and worshipers of God. These are all synagogues of Satan. Satan presides over them and works in them, and his interests are served by them. He receives horrid homage and honor from them.

Second, for **a synagogue of Satan** to pretend that it is the church or the Israel of God is nothing short of blasphemy. God is greatly dishonored when his name is made use of to promote and patronize Satan's interests. He greatly resents this blasphemy and will take just revenge on those who persist in it.

d. God knows in advance about the trials his people will suffer, and he warns them about these trials before they take place, and so arms them against them.

(1) He forewarns them about future trials. **I tell you, the devil will put some of you in prison to test you** (verse 10). God's people must expect a succession of troubles in this world, and their troubles usually become greater and greater. They had been impoverished through their **afflictions** (verse 9) previously, and now they are going to be imprisoned. Notice that it is **the devil** who stirs up his followers, wicked people, to persecute God's people. Tyrants and persecutors are the devil's tools, even though they may gratify their own sinful malevolence and not realize they are motivated by diabolical malice.

(2) Christ forearms them against the approaching troubles.

First, he does this by his counsel: **Do not be afraid of what you are about to suffer** (verse 10). This is not just a word of command but of efficacy, not only forbidding slavish fear (**do not be afraid**), but subduing it, and so furnishing the soul with strength and courage.

Second, Christ shows them how their sufferings will be alleviated and limited. In the first place, their sufferings will not be universal. This suffering is restricted to **some** of them. **Some** of them, not all of them, would be thrown into prison. These people will be those who are best able to endure this, and they might expect to be visited and comforted by the rest. In the second place, they will not be in prison forever but for a set time, a short time, **ten days.** This would not be an everlasting tribulation. "If the Lord had not cut short those days, no one would survive. But for the sake of the elect, whom he has chosen, he has shortened them" (Mark 13:20). In the third place, these tribulations are to **test** them, not to destroy them, so that their faith and patience and courage might be proved and improved and be found to honor and glorify God.

Third, Christ proposes and promises a glorious reward for their faithfulness: **Be faithful, even to the point of death, and I will give you the crown of life** (verse 10). Observe, in the first place, the certainty of the reward: **I will give you.** Christ has said it, and he is able to do it. He has promised that he will do it. They will receive the reward from his own hand, and none of his enemies will be able to grab it from him. In the second place, note the suitability of this reward. It is a **crown,** to reward their poverty, their faithfulness, and their conflict. Not only is it a crown, but it is **the crown of life,** to reward those who have been **faithful, even to the point of death.** It is a crown for those who are faithful until they die, to those who lay down their lives in faithfulness to Christ. That life, so worn out in his service or laid down in his cause, will be rewarded with another, much better **life** that will be eternal.

3. The conclusion of this message, as before, is:

a. A call to universal attention, that all people, all the world, should hear what passes between Christ and his churches. This includes how he commends them, how he comforts them, how he reproves their failures, how he rewards their faithfulness. All the inhabitants of the world should observe God's dealings with his own people. The whole world can learn wisdom in this way.

b. With a gracious promise to the conquering Christian: **He who has an ear, let him hear what the Spirit says to the churches. He who overcomes will not be hurt at all by the second death** (verse 11). Notice that:

(1) There is not only a first but a **second death;** a death after the body is dead.

(2) This **second death** is indescribably worse than the first death, both in the dying pangs and in its agonies. For these agonies are the agonies of

the soul, which has no support, and these agonies are in its duration. It is *eternal* death. It is fatally harmful to all who fall under it.

(3) From this harmful, destructive death, Christ will save all his faithful servants. The **second death** will have no power over those who take part in the first resurrection. The first death will not hurt them; the **second death** will have no power over them.

Verses 12-17

To the angel of the church in Pergamum write:
These are the words of him who has the sharp, double-edged sword. I know where you live—where Satan has his throne. Yet you remain true to my name. You did not renounce your faith in me, even in the days of Antipas, my faithful witness, who was put to death in your city—where Satan lives.

Nevertheless, I have a few things against you: You have people there who hold to the teaching of Balaam, who taught Balak to entice the Israelites to sin by eating food sacrificed to idols and by committing sexual immorality. Likewise you also have those who hold to the teaching of the Nicolaitans. Repent therefore! Otherwise, I will soon come to you and will fight against them with the sword of my mouth.

He who has an ear, let him hear what the Spirit says to the churches. To him who overcomes, I will give some of the hidden manna. I will also give him a white stone with a new name written on it, known only to him who receives it.

Here we also consider:

1. The inscription of this passage.

a. Who it was sent to: **To the angel of the church of Pergamum** (verse 12). Whether this was a city raised up out of the ruins of old Troy, a New Troy (as London was once called), or some other city of the same name is neither certain nor material. It was a place where Christ had called and constituted a church through the preaching of the Gospel and the grace of his Spirit making the Word effective.

b. Who it was that sent this message to Pergamum: the same Jesus who here describes himself as one **who has the sharp, double-edged sword** (verse 12). "Out of his mouth came a sharp double-edged sword" (1:16).

Some commentators have observed that in the different titles of Christ attached to the beginning of several of these letters, there is something specifically applicable to the state of those churches. So, for example, in the letter to Ephesus, what could be more pertinent to wake up a sleepy and declining church than to hear of Christ as the one who "holds the seven stars in his right hand and walks among the seven golden lampstands" (2:1)?

The church in Pergamum was infested with people of corrupt minds, who did what they could to corrupt the faith and behavior of the church.

Christ, resolved to fight against them through the sword of his Word, takes the title of the one who **has the sharp, double-edged sword.**

(1) The Word of God is a **sword.** It is both a defensive and an offensive weapon. It is, in God's hand, able to kill both sin and sinners.

(2) It is a **sharp** sword. No heart is too hard to be wounded by it, and no knot is so tightly tied that it cannot be severed. It can cut through and separate the soul and the spirit—that is, between the soul and those sinful actions that through habit become another soul or seem to be essential to it.

(3) It is a **double-edged** sword. It turns and cuts every way. There is the edge of the law against those who break that dispensation and the edge of the Gospel against those who despise that dispensation. There is an edge that can wound and an edge to open a festered wound in order to bring healing. There is no escape from the edge of this sword. If you turn to the right side, it has an edge on that side; if you turn to the left side, you fall on the edge of the sword on that side. It turns every way.

2. From the inscription we move on to the contents of this letter, in which the method is very similar to the other letters.

a. Christ takes notice of the trials and difficulties this church encountered. **I know where you live—where Satan has his throne. Yet you remain true to my name. You did not renounce your faith in me, even in the days of Antipas, my faithful witness, who was put to death in your city— where Satan lives** (verse 13). The deeds of God's servants are best known when the circumstances under which they did those deeds are carefully considered. The circumstance that added great luster to the good deeds of this church was the place where it was planted, a place **where Satan has his throne.** As our great Lord takes notice of all the advantages and opportunities we have for duty in the places we live in, so he takes notice of all the temptations and discouragements we meet with in the places where we live. He takes all this into account and makes the necessary allowances.

This people lived **where Satan has his throne,** where he held court. His circuit is throughout the world; his **throne** is in places that are notorious for wickedness, error, and cruelty. Some think the Roman governor of this city was violently opposed to the Christians, so that the center of persecution was Satan's **throne.**

b. Christ commends their steadfastness: **Yet you remain true to my name. You did not renounce your faith in me.** These two expressions mean the same thing. The former may signify the effect, the latter the cause or means.

(1) **You remain true to my name.** "You are not ashamed of your relationship to me, but count it an honor that **my name** is placed upon you. Just as the wife bears the husband's name, so you are called by **my name. You remain true** in this and count it an honor and privilege."

(2) "What has made you faithful is the grace of **faith.**" People who **renounce** their **faith** may boast about their sincerity and their faithfulness

to God and their consciences. But it is most rare for those who let go of the true faith to retain their faithfulness. Faith is the rock on which most people make shipwreck of their lives, and shipwreck of their good consciences too. Here our blessed Lord praises the faithfulness of this church in the context of the circumstances of the times, as well as of where they lived. They had been steadfast **even in the days of Antipas, my faithful witness.** Who this person was, and whether there is anything mysterious in his name, we have no definite information. But we do know he was Christ's faithful disciple, for which he suffered martyrdom. He sealed his faith and faithfulness with his blood in the place **where Satan has his throne.** And although the rest of the believers knew this and saw it, they were not put off but remained faithful. This is mentioned to their credit.

c. Christ reproves them for their sinful failures. **Nevertheless, I have a few things against you: You have people there who hold to the teaching of Balaam, who taught Balak to entice the Israelites to sin by eating food sacrificed to idols and by committing sexual immorality** (verse 14). Some people taught that it was lawful to eat **food sacrificed to idols** and that **sexual immorality** was not sinful. These people, through their impure worship, drew people into impure practices, as Balaam did to the Israelites. Notice:

(1) An impure spirit and an impure flesh often go together. Corrupt doctrines and corrupt worship often lead to corrupt behavior.

(2) It is right to call the followers of any heresy by the original leader's name. It is the easiest way to identify them.

(3) To maintain fellowship with people of corrupt principles and behavior displeases God and brings guilt and darkness on the whole of society. They take part in the sins of other people. Though the church as such has no power to punish these people, either for heresy or immorality, with physical punishment, it does have the power to exclude them from Holy Communion. If the church does not do this, then Christ, the Head and Lawgiver of the church, will be displeased with it.

d. Christ calls them to repentance: **Repent therefore! Otherwise, I will soon come to you and will fight against them with the sword of my mouth.** Notice here:

(1) Repentance is the duty of saints as well as sinners. It is a gospel duty.

(2) It is the duty of churches and communities as well as of individuals. Those who sin together should repent together.

(3) It is the duty of Christian societies to repent of other people's sins, insofar as they have been involved in them.

(4) When God comes to punish the corrupt members of a church, he rebukes that church itself for allowing them to continue in its fellowship, and some drops of the storm fall upon that whole society.

(5) No sword cuts so deep, nor inflicts such a mortal wound, as the sword of Christ's mouth—**the sword of my mouth.** Just allow the threats of the Word to home in on the conscience of a sinner and he will quickly

be a terror to himself. If these threats are executed, then the sinner will be cut off completely. The Word of God will take hold of the sinner sooner or later, either for his conviction or for his confusion.

3. We have the conclusion of this letter, where, after the usual command for worldwide attention, there is the promise of great favor to those who overcome: **He who has an ear, let him hear what the Spirit says to the churches. To him who overcomes, I will give some of the hidden manna. I will also give him a white stone with a new name written on it, known only to him who receives it** (verse 17).

a. **The hidden manna** indicates the influences and comforts of the Spirit of Christ in communion with the believer, coming down from heaven into the soul from time to time for its support, to let it have a little taste of how saints and angels live in heaven. This is **hidden** from the rest of the world. "Each heart knows its own bitterness, and no one else can share its joy" (Proverbs 14:10). This delight is contained in Christ, our ark of the covenant, in the holy of holies.

b. The **white stone with** its **new name written on it** is absolution from the guilt of sin, alluding to the ancient custom of giving a **white stone** to those acquitted after a trial, and a black stone to those condemned. The **new name** is the name of adoption. Adopted people take the name of the family into which they are adopted. Nobody can read the evidence of a person's adoption except for the person who is adopted. Even he cannot always read it. But if he perseveres, he will have both the evidence of being a child of God and of the inheritance.

Verses 18-29

To the angel of the church in Thyatira write:

These are the words of the Son of God, whose eyes are like blazing fire and whose feet are like burnished bronze. I know your deeds, your love and faith, your service and perseverance, and that you are now doing more than you did at first.

Nevertheless, I have this against you: You tolerate that woman Jezebel, who calls herself a prophetess. By her teaching she misleads my servants into sexual immorality and the eating of food sacrificed to idols. I have given her time to repent of her immorality, but she is unwilling. So I will cast her on a bed of suffering, and I will make those who commit adultery with her suffer intensely, unless they repent of her ways. I will strike her children dead. Then all the churches will know that I am he who searches hearts and minds, and I will repay each of you according to your deeds. Now I say to the rest of you in Thyatira, to you who do not hold to her teaching and have not learned Satan's so-called deep secrets (I will not impose any other burden on you): Only hold on to what you have until I come.

To him who overcomes and does my will to the end, I will give authority over the nations—

"He will rule them with an iron scepter; he will dash them to pieces like pottery"—just as I have received authority from my Father. I will also give him the morning star. He who has an ear, let him hear what the Spirit says to the churches.

The form of each letter is very much the same. In this letter, like the other letters, we have to consider the inscription, contents, and conclusion.

1. The inscription tells us:

a. To whom the letter is addressed: **To the angel of the church in Thyatira** (verse 18). **Thyatira** was a city in the proconsulate of Asia, bordering Mysia on the north and the trading town of Lydia on the south. A woman called Lydia, who traded in purple cloth, came from Thyatira. When she was in Philippi, most probably on business, she was converted after she heard Paul speak.

On the Sabbath we went outside the city gate to the river, where we expected to find a place of prayer. We sat down and began to speak to the women who had gathered there. One of those listening was a woman named Lydia, a dealer in purple cloth from the city of Thyatira, who was a worshiper of God. The Lord opened her heart to respond to Paul's message. When she and the members of her household were baptized, she invited us to her home. "If you consider me a believer in the Lord," she said, "come and stay at my house." And she persuaded us.

—Acts 16:13-15

It is not known if the Gospel spread to Thyatira through Lydia. But this letter does assure us that it was there and had formed a successful gospel-church.

b. By whom it was sent: **the Son of God** (verse 18). He is described here as having **eyes . . . like blazing fire and . . . feet . . . like burnished bronze.** His general title here is **Son of God,** that is, the eternal, one and only Son of God. This denotes that he has the same nature as the Father but a distinct and subordinate manner of subsistence.

(1) That his **eyes are like blazing fire** signifies his piercing, penetrating, perfect knowledge. He has a thorough insight into all people and into all things. **I am he who searches hearts and minds** (2:23). He will make all the churches aware that he does this.

(2) His **feet are like burnished bronze.** This indicates that the results of his providence are awe-inspiring and are characterized by steadfastness, purity, and holiness. As Christ judges with perfect wisdom, so he acts with perfect strength and steadiness.

2. The contents, or subject matter, of this letter, like the others, include:

a. The honorable character and commendation Christ gives to his church, ministry, and people. This is given by someone who is no stranger to them, but who is well-known to them and knows the motives that have governed their actions. About this church Christ makes honorable mention of:

(1) Their charity. **I know your deeds, your love and faith, your service and perseverance, and that you are now doing more than you did at first.** (verse 19). In general, they have a disposition to do good to all people and in particular to the household of faith. There is no religion where charity is absent.

(2) Their **service.** This is mentioned with particular reference to the officers of the church. "The elders who direct the affairs of the church well are worthy of double honor, especially those whose work is preaching and teaching" (1 Timothy 5:17).

(3) Their **faith,** which actuated all the rest, both their **love** and their **service.**

(4) Their **perseverance.** People who are most charitable to others, most diligent in their own work, and most faithful must still expect to meet with circumstances that will demand **perseverance.**

(5) Their growing fruitfulness. **You are now doing more than you did at first.** This is an excellent characteristic. When others had lost their first love and their first zeal, these people were growing wiser and better. It should be the ambition and earnest desire of all Christians that their last deeds should be their best deeds, that they may be better and better every day, and that their last day is their best day.

b. A faithful reproof for what was amiss. This is not so directly charged on the church itself as on some wicked people among them who had seduced them. The church was at fault for conniving too much with them. These wicked seducers are called by Jezebel's name and compared with her: **Nevertheless, I have this against you: You tolerate that woman Jezebel, who calls herself a prophetess. By her teaching she misleads my servants into sexual immorality and the eating of food sacrificed to idols. I have given her time to repent of her immorality, but she is unwilling** (verses 20-21). Jezebel persecuted the Lord's prophets and was a great patroness of idolaters and false prophets. These seducers sinned by attempting to lure God's **servants into sexual immorality** and into **the eating of food sacrificed to idols.** They called themselves prophets, and Jezebel called herself a **prophetess,** thus claiming superior authority to the ministers in that church.

Two things aggravated the sin of these seducers who, being one in their spirit and design, are spoken of as one person.

(1) They made use of the name of God to oppose the truth of his doctrine and worship. This greatly compounded their sin.

(2) They abused God's patience by hardening themselves in their wickedness. God gave them **time to repent,** but they were **unwilling.** Observe, in the first place, that repentance is necessary to prevent the sin-

ner's ruin. In the second place, repentance requires a course of time and an appropriate opportunity. In the third place, when God gives the opportunity for repentance, he expects to see the appropriate fruits of repentance. "Produce fruit in keeping with repentance" (Matthew 3:8). In the fourth place, when the opportunity for repentance is lost, the sinner perishes with double destruction.

Why should the wickedness of this Jezebel be leveled against the church of Thyatira? Because that church allowed her to seduce the people of that city. But how could they have avoided this? They did not have the civic power, as a church, to banish or imprison her. But they did have the ministerial power to censure and excommunicate her. It is probable that failing to use the power they had made them share in her sin.

c. The punishment of this seducer, this **Jezebel: So I will cast her on a bed of suffering, and I will make those who commit adultery with her suffer intensely, unless they repent of her ways. I will strike her children dead. Then all the churches will know that I am he who searches hearts and minds, and I will repay each of you according to your deeds** (verses 22-23). In these words is hidden a prediction of the fall of spiritual Babylon.

(1) **I will cast her on a bed of suffering,** not of pleasure, a bed of flames. And those who have sinned with her will suffer with her. But this can be prevented through repentance.

(2) **I will strike her children dead,** that is, with "the second death" (2:11). This second death does the work effectively and leaves no hope of future life and no resurrection for those who are killed by it, but only shame and everlasting contempt.

d. Christ's purpose in the destruction of these wicked seducers. This is contained in his instruction of others, especially of his churches. **Then all the churches will know that I am he who searches hearts and minds, and I will repay each of you according to your deeds.** "The LORD is known by his justice" (Psalm 9:16). Through the revenge he takes on the seducers, Christ will make known:

(1) His infallible knowledge of people's **hearts** and motives. He knows their indifference and their inclination to side with idolaters.

(2) His impartial justice: **I will repay each of you according to your deeds.** Just being called Christians will offer them no protection. Their churches should not be sanctuaries for sin and sinners.

e. The encouragement given to those who kept themselves pure and undefiled. **Now I say to the rest of you in Thyatira, to you who do not hold to her teaching and have not learned Satan's so-called deep secrets (I will not impose any other burden on you) . . .** (verse 24). Notice:

(1) What these seducers called their doctrines: **deep secrets,** profound mysteries. They attracted the people and tried to persuade them that they had a deeper insight into religion than their own ministers could give them.

(2) What Christ called them: **Satan's so-called deep secrets.** Christ labeled them as satanic delusions and diabolic mysteries. There is indeed a mystery of iniquity: "For the secret power of lawlessness is already at work" (2 Thessalonians 2:7). There is also the mystery of godliness: "Beyond all question, the mystery of godliness is great" (1 Timothy 3:16). It is dangerous to despise God's mysteries, and it is dangerous to welcome Satan's mysteries.

(3) How tender Christ is toward his faithful servants: **To him who overcomes and does my will to the end, I will give authority over the nations** (verse 26). "I will not burden your faith with any new mysteries, nor your consciences with any new laws. I only require you to pay attention to what you have received. Do **my will to the end.** I desire nothing else." Christ is coming to put an end to all the temptations of his people. If they remain faithful and keep their consciences clear until he comes, all the difficulties and dangers are past.

3. We now come to the conclusion. **To him who overcomes and does my will to the end, I will give authority over the nations—"He will rule them with an iron scepter; he will dash them to pieces like pottery"— just as I have received authority from my Father. I will also give him the morning star. He who has an ear, let him hear what the Spirit says to the churches** (verses 26-29). Here we have:

a. The promise of an ample reward to the persevering, victorious believer. This is shown in two parts.

(1) Very great power and dominion over the rest of the world. **Authority over the nations** may refer either to the time when the empire became Christian and the world was under the rule of a Christian emperor, as in Constantine's time; or to the other world when believers will sit down with Christ on his judgment throne. The latter is the time when they will join Christ in putting on trial, condemning, and sentencing enemies of Christ and of his church. "The upright will rule over them in the morning" (Psalm 49:14).

(2) Knowledge and wisdom, suitable for such power and dominion: **I will also give him the morning star.** Christ is **the morning star.** He brings day with him into the soul, the light of grace and glory, and he will give his people that perfection of light and wisdom that is appropriate for the state of dignity and dominion that they will have on the morning of the resurrection.

b. This letter concludes with the usual demand to be listened to: **He who has an ear, let him hear what the Spirit says to the churches.** In the previous letters this command precedes a concluding promise. But in this letter, and in all the following letters, it comes after the promise and tells us that we should all take note of the promises, as well as of the precepts, that Christ delivers to the churches.

Revelation
Chapter 3

Verses 1-6

To the angel of the church in Sardis write:

These are the words of him who holds the seven spirits of God and the seven stars. I know your deeds; you have a reputation of being alive, but you are dead. Wake up! Strengthen what remains and is about to die, for I have not found your deeds complete in the sight of my God. Remember, therefore, what you have received and heard; obey it, and repent. But if you do not wake up, I will come like a thief, and you will not know at what time I will come to you.

Yet you have a few people in Sardis who have not soiled their clothes. They will walk with me, dressed in white, for they are worthy. He who overcomes will, like them, be dressed in white. I will never erase his name from the book of life, but will acknowledge his name before my Father and his angels. He who has an ear, let him hear what the Spirit says to the churches.

Here is:

1. The preface, showing:

a. To whom this letter is written: **To the angel of the church in Sardis** (verse 1). Sardis, an ancient city of Lydia, on the banks of Mount Tmolus, is said to have been the chief city of Asia the Less. It was the first city in that part of the world that was converted through the preaching of St. John. Some people believe it was the first city to protest against Christianity, and one of the first to become a ruin. It remains a ruin to this day, with no church or ministry.

b. By whom this message was sent. The description of the Lord Jesus as he who **holds the seven spirits of God and the seven stars** (verse 1) comes from 1:4 ("the seven spirits before his throne").

(1) Christ has **seven spirits**. This refers to the Holy Spirit with his various powers, graces, and methods of working. He is personally one,

though effective in a variety of ways. In that sense he may be said to be **seven**. This is also the number of the churches written to and of the angels of the churches. This indicates that every minister and every church has a dispensation and measure of the Spirit, from which they can benefit. This is a stock of spiritual influence for that minister and church so that it can increase in size and continue to exist. This measure of the Spirit is not normally taken away, unless the believers forfeit it through neglect or misuse. Churches have their spiritual stock and fund as well as particular believers. This letter is being sent to a languishing ministry and church. So it is highly appropriate that the believers there should be reminded about **the seven spirits of God**, the Spirit without measure. This is the perfect Spirit, from whom they may receive help to revive the spiritual work among them.

(2) He **holds . . . the seven stars**. These are the angels of the churches. They are appointed by Christ to do their work, and they are accountable to Christ, which should make them faithful and zealous. Christ has ministers to work for him and spiritual influences to communicate to his ministers for the good of the church. The Holy Spirit usually works through this ministry, and this ministry would be useless without the Spirit. The same divine hand holds them both.

2. The contents of the letter. It can be observed in this letter that whereas in the other letters Christ starts by commending what was good in the churches and then proceeds to tell them what was wrong, in this (and in the letter to Laodicea) he begins:

a. With a rebuke, and a very severe one: **I know your deeds; you have a reputation of being alive, but you are dead** (verse 1). Hypocrisy and a lamentable decay in religion are the sins this church is accused of. Her accuser knows her well and knows all about her deeds.

(1) This church had won a great reputation. It had a name, and a very honorable name, for being a flourishing church. It had a name for vital, living religion, for purity of doctrine, unity among its members, uniformity in worship, decency, and order. We do not read about any unhappy divisions among them. Everything appeared to be well as far as people could observe.

(2) But this church was not in reality what it was by reputation. They had a **reputation of being alive but** were **dead**, "having a form of godliness but denying its power" (2 Timothy 3:5). They had a name for being alive but did not possess the principle of life. If they were not completely dead, there was a great deadness about their souls and in their services. There was a great deadness in the spirits of their ministers and in their acts of ministry, in their praying, in their preaching, and in their conversations. What little life was left among them was on the verge of expiring. They were on the verge of death.

b. Our Lord proceeds to give this degenerate church the best advice:

Wake up! Strengthen what remains and is about to die, for I have not found your deeds complete in the sight of my God (verse 2).

(1) Christ advises them to be watchful. Their sinful deadness had been caused by their lack of watchfulness. Whenever we are off guard, we lose ground and therefore must return to our watchfulness against sin and Satan and whatever destroys the life and power of godliness.

(2) **Strengthen what remains and is about to die.** Some commentators think this refers to people. There were a few people who had maintained their integrity, but they were in danger of declining like the rest. It is difficult to maintain a life of power and godliness ourselves when we see deadness all around us. Or this verse may refer not to people, but to practices, for the verse continues, **for I have not found your deeds complete in the sight of my God.** There was something lacking in their deeds. They had the shell, but the kernel was missing. They had the body, but no soul; they had the shadow, but no substance. The inward thing was lacking. Their deeds were hollow and empty. Prayers were not supported by holy desires, the giving of money was not backed up with true charity, and sabbaths were not full of suitable devotion of the soul toward God. They did not have the inward affections to match their outward deeds. Where the Spirit is lacking, the form does not last long.

(3) To recollect themselves. **Remember, therefore, what you have received and heard; obey it, and repent** (verse 3). They had to **remember** what they had **received and heard** from God, how they had received God's mercy on their souls at the beginning. They had to remember what affections they had felt as they received the Word and the ordinances, the love from their Christian friends, the kindness of their youth, and how they had felt as they welcomed the Gospel and grace of God. Where had the blessedness they had then spoken about gone?

(4) In order to hold on to what they had received, so that they might not lose everything, they had to **repent.** They had to **repent** sincerely so that they did not lose so much of their spiritual life and run the risk of losing it all.

c. Christ emphasizes his counsel with a dreadful threat, to ensure that his warning is heeded: **But if you do not wake up, I will come like a thief, and you will not know at what time I will come to you** (verse 3). Observe:

(1) When Christ withdraws his gracious presence from a people, he comes to them in judgment. His judicial presence will be very dreadful for those who have caused his gracious presence to be removed because of their sin.

(2) His judicial approach to a dead, declining people will come as a surprise. Their deadness is their security, and as it causes an angry visit from Christ, it will stop them from anticipating it and preparing for it.

(3) Such a visit from Christ will be to their loss. He **will come like a**

thief. He will strip them of their remaining enjoyments and mercies—not by fraud, but in justice and righteousness.

d. Our blessed Lord does not leave this sinful people without some comfort and encouragement. In the middle of judgment he remembers mercy: **Yet you have a few people in Sardis who have not soiled their clothes. They will walk with me, dressed in white, for they are worthy** (verse 4). Note here:

(1) Christ makes honorable mention of the faithful remnant in Sardis, even though it is small: **Yet you have a few people in Sardis who have not soiled their clothes.** They have not given in to the prevailing corruptions and pollution of the day and of the place in which they lived. God takes notice of the smallest number of those who abide with him. The fewer they are, the more precious is their faithfulness in his sight.

(2) He makes a very gracious promise to them: **They will walk with me, dressed in white, for they are worthy.** Their white clothes symbolize justification, adoption, and comfort. Alternatively, white could stand for robes of honor and glory in the coming world. **They will walk with** Christ in the pleasant walks of the heavenly paradise. And what delightful conversation there will be between Christ and them when they walk together in this way. This honor suits their integrity, which their faithfulness has prepared them for and which it is not at all unbecoming for Christ to bestow on them. This is not a legal requirement but a gospel-worthiness that is ascribed to them. It is not merit but meetness. Those who walk with Christ in the clean clothes of genuine practical holiness here, keeping themselves unpolluted from the world, will walk with Christ in white robes of honor and glory in the coming world. This is a suitable reward. "Religion that God our Father accepts as pure and faultless is this: to look after orphans and widows in their distress and to keep oneself from being polluted by the world" (James 1:27).

3. We now come to the conclusion of this letter. As before, we have:

a. A great reward promised to the conquering Christian. **He who overcomes will, like them, be dressed in white. I will never erase his name from the book of life, but will acknowledge his name before my Father and his angels** (verse 5). This is very similar to what has already been mentioned: **He who overcomes will, like them, be dressed in white.** The purity of grace will be rewarded with the purity of glory. Holiness, when perfected, will be its own reward. Glory is the perfection of grace, differing not in kind, but in degree. To this is added another very suitable promise: **I will never erase his name from the book of life, but will acknowledge his name before my Father and his angels.** Notice:

(1) Christ has his **book of life,** his register and roll of all who will inherit eternal life. It is a book of eternal election. It is also a book of remembrance of all those who have lived for God and have kept up the life and power of godliness through evil times.

(2) Christ **will never erase his name.** The Savior will not blot out the names of his chosen and faithful ones from this **book of life.** People may be enrolled in the registers of the church, as baptized, as making a profession of faith, as having a name of being alive. But this name may be blotted out of the register when it appears to be just a name and to be devoid of spiritual life. Such people often lose even the name of being a follower of Christ before they die. They leave God to blot their name from the book of life because of their great and open wickedness. But the names of those who overcome will never be blotted out.

(3) Christ will produce this **book of life** and will **acknowledge** the names of the faithful who stand before God—**before my Father and his angels.** Christ will do this as their Judge. "And I saw the dead, great and small, standing before the throne, and books were opened. Another book was opened, which is the book of life. The dead were judged according to what they had done as recorded in the books" (Revelation 20:12). He will do that as their Captain and Head, leading them with him triumphantly to heaven, presenting them to the Father. How great this honor and reward will be!

b. The command of universal attention concludes this message: **He who has an ear, let him hear what the Spirit says to the churches** (verse 6). People should give due attention to every word from God. What may seem to be particularly appropriate to one group of people has something instructive to say to everyone.

Verses 7-13

To the angel of the church in Philadelphia write:
These are the words of him who is holy and true, who holds the key of David. What he opens, no one can shut; and what he shuts, no one can open. I know your deeds. See, I have placed before you an open door that no one can shut. I know that you have little strength, yet you have kept my word and have not denied my name. I will make those who are of the synagogue of Satan, who claim to be Jews though they are not, but are liars—I will make them come and fall down at your feet and acknowledge that I have loved you. Since you have kept my command to endure patiently, I will also keep you from the hour of trial that is going to come upon the whole world to test those who live on the earth.
I am coming soon. Hold on to what you have, so that no one will take your crown. Him who overcomes I will make a pillar in the temple of my God. Never again will he leave it. I will write on him the name of my God and the name of the city of my God, the new Jerusalem, which is coming down out of heaven from my God; and I

will also write on him my new name. He who has an ear, let him hear what the Spirit says to the churches.

We come now to the sixth letter sent to one of the churches of Asia. We notice:

1. The inscription, showing:

a. Who it was originally sent to: **To the angel of the church in Philadelphia** (verse 7). This also was a city in Asia Minor, bordering Mysia and Lydia. It derives its name **Philadelphia** from the brotherly love for which it was renowned. We can hardly imagine that it was given its name after Christianity had been established in it. It is most unlikely to have derived its name from the Christian love that all believers have and should have for each other, since they are the Father's children and Christ's brothers and sisters. Rather, **Philadelphia** was an ancient name and came about because of the love and kindness that its citizens had shown to each other. This was an excellent spirit and, when sanctified by the grace of the Gospel, would make the believers there an excellent church, as indeed they were. No fault was found with this church. There were doubtless faults there on account of their common infirmity, but love covers such faults.

b. By whom this letter was signed. This letter is from the same Jesus who is alone the universal Head of all the churches. Observe here the title by which he chooses to represent himself to this church: **These are the words of him who is holy and true, who holds the key of David. What he opens, no one can shut; and what he shuts, no one can open** (verse 7). We see here Christ's personal character: he is **holy and true.** His nature is **holy**, and therefore he cannot but be **true** to his word, for he has spoken in his holiness. Another aspect of his character is that he **holds the key of David. What he opens, no one can shut; and what he shuts, no one can open.** Christ has the **key** of the house of David, the **key** of government and authority in and over the church.

(1) Notice the acts of his government. First, **he opens.** He opens a door of opportunity to his churches. He opens a door of utterance to his ministers. He opens a door of admission into the visible church, laying down the terms of fellowship, and he opens the door of admission into the church triumphant, according to the terms of salvation that he has laid down.

Second, he **shuts** the door. When Christ pleases, he shuts the door of opportunity and the door of utterance and leaves obstinate sinners shut up in the hardness of their hearts. He shuts the door of church fellowship against unbelievers and profane people, and he shuts the door of heaven against the foolish widows who have slept away their day of grace and against evildoers, no matter how vain and confident they may be.

(2) The way he carries out these acts. He does this with absolute sovereignty, independent of the will of people, who are powerless to resist him. **What he opens, no one can shut; and what he shuts, no one can open.**

He works to will and to do, and when he works, no one can oppose him. These were appropriate characteristics for him when he was speaking to a church that had tried to be conformed to Christ in holiness and truth and that had enjoyed a wide door of freedom and opportunity under his care and rule.

2. The contents of this letter, showing:

a. Christ's reminder of what he had done for them. **I know your deeds. See, I have placed before you an open door that no one can shut. I know that you have little strength, yet you have kept my word and have not denied my name** (verse 8). "I have set it open, and I have kept it open despite many adversaries." Learn here:

(1) Christ is to be acknowledged as the Author of all the freedom and opportunity his churches enjoy.

(2) Christ takes note and keeps a record of how long he has preserved their spiritual freedoms and privileges for them.

(3) Wicked people envy God's people's door of freedom and would gladly close it against them.

(4) If we do not provoke Christ to shut this door against us, people are unable to do this.

b. This church is corrected but not condemned: **I know that you have little strength, yet you have kept my word and have not denied my name.** There seems to be a gentle rebuke hidden here. "**You have little strength,** a little grace; though it is not in proportion with the wide door of opportunity that I have opened up for you, you still have genuine grace, and this has kept you faithful." Genuine grace, though weak, has the divine approval. While Christ accepts a **little strength,** believers should not be satisfied with a **little.** They should strive to grow in grace and to be strong in faith, giving glory to God. "Grow in the grace and knowledge of our Lord and Savior Jesus Christ. To him be glory both now and forever! Amen" (2 Peter 3:18).

Genuine grace, though weak, will do more than the greatest gifts or highest degrees of common grace, as it enables the Christian to keep Christ's Word and not to deny his name. Obedience, faithfulness, and an open confession of Christ's name are the fruits of true grace and as such please Christ.

c. Here is a promise about the great favors God wants to bestow on his church: **I will make those who are of the synagogue of Satan, who claim to be Jews though they are not, but are liars—I will make them come and fall down at your feet and acknowledge that I have loved you** (verse 9). This favor is made up of two things:

(1) Christ would make this church's enemies subject to her. First, these enemies are described as people **who claim to be Jews though they are not.** They lied in this claim. They pretended to be the only and special people of God when in reality they were members of **the synagogue of**

Satan. Although they profess to be the only people of God, their profession is a lie: they **are liars.**

Their subjection to the church is then described: **I will make them come and fall down at your feet.** They will not pay a religious or divine honor to the church itself or to its ministry, but will be convinced that they have been wrong, that this church is in the right and is loved by Christ, and they will want to be taken into communion with her, so that they may worship the same God in the same way. How is this great change going to be brought about? By God's power working in the hearts of his enemies, and through the discoveries of his special favor to his church. **I will make them . . . acknowledge that I have loved you.** Notice in the first place that the greatest honor and happiness any church can enjoy consists in the special love and favor of Christ. In the second place Christ can disclose his favor to his people in such a way that their enemies will see it and be forced to acknowledge it. In the third place this will, by Christ's grace, soften the hearts of their enemies and make them wish to be admitted into fellowship with them.

(2) Another example of the favor Christ promises to this church is persevering grace in the most trying times: **Since you have kept my command to endure patiently, I will also keep you from the hour of trial that is going to come upon the whole world to test those who live on the earth** (verse 10). This is the reward for their previous faithfulness. "For with the measure you use, it will be measured to you" (Luke 6:38). Notice here, first, that the Gospel of Christ is the word of his patience: **Since you have kept my command to endure patiently.** This is the fruit of God's patience to a sinful world. It sets before people the exemplary patience of Christ in all his sufferings for them. It calls those who receive it to exercise patience just as Christ did. Second, this Gospel should be carefully kept by everyone who enjoys it. They must keep the faith, practice, and worship laid down in the Gospel.

Third, after a day of exercising patience, we must expect an hour of temptation. A day of gospel-peace and freedom is a day of God's patience, which can hardly be improved on, and therefore it is often followed by an hour of trial and temptation. Fourth, sometimes the trial is more general and universal. It comes on the whole world, and when it is general in this way, it usually does not last so long. Fifth, those who keep the Gospel during a time of peace will be kept by Christ in the hour of temptation. By keeping the Gospel they are prepared for the trial. The same divine grace that made them fruitful in times of peace will make them faithful in times of persecution.

d. Christ calls the church to undertake the duty that he had previously promised he would enable them to carry out—that is, to persevere. **I am coming soon. Hold on to what you have, so that no one will take your crown** (verse 11).

(1) The duty itself: **Hold on to what you have**—faith, truth, strength of grace, zeal, love for the brethren. "You have possessed that excellent treasure; hold on to it."

(2) The motives taken from the sudden appearance of Christ. **I am coming soon.** "See, I am coming to relieve those who are being tried, to reward their faithfulness, and to punish those who fall away. They will lose that crown they once seemed to have a right to, that they had hoped for and were happy to think about." The persevering Christian will win the prize from backsliding people who merely profess the Christian faith, who once also stood to win the prize.

3. The conclusion of the letter: **Him who overcomes I will make a pillar in the temple of my God. Never again will he leave it. I will write on him the name of my God and the name of the city of my God, the new Jerusalem, which is coming down out of heaven from my God; and I will also write on him my new name** (verse 12). Here, in his usual way, our Saviour promises a glorious reward to the victorious believer, in two ways:

a. He shall be a monument, **a pillar in the temple.** Heaven needs no such props, but he will be a monument of the free and powerful grace of God, a monument that will never be defaced or removed, as the many stately pillars erected in honor of the Roman emperors and generals were.

b. On this monumental pillar there will be an honorable inscription, as is usual in such cases.

(1) **The name of my God.** It will have the name of God, in whose cause the believer lived, whom he served, and for whom he suffered in this warfare. It will also have inscribed on it **the name of the city of my God**, the church of God, **the new Jerusalem, which is coming down out of heaven from my God.** On this pillar will be recorded all the services the believer did for God's church, how he asserted her rights, enlarged her borders, and maintained her purity and honor. This will be a greater name than Asiaticus or Africanus. It will be the name of a soldier who served in God's army in the wars of the church.

(2) **My new name.** Christ's new name is the Mediator, the Redeemer, the Captain of salvation. From this it will be clear under whose banner this conquering believer enlisted, at whose command he fought, by whose example he was encouraged, and under whose influence he fought the good fight and became victorious. "Fight the good fight of the faith" (1 Timothy 6:12).

The letter concludes with a command that it should be taken notice of: **He who has an ear, let him hear what the Spirit says to the churches** (verse 13). How Christ loves and values his faithful people; how he commends, and how he will crown their faithfulness!

47

Verses 14-22

To the angel of the church in Laodicea write:

These are the words of the Amen, the faithful and true witness, the ruler of God's creation. I know your deeds, that you are neither cold nor hot. I wish you were either one or the other! So, because you are lukewarm—neither hot nor cold—I am about to spit you out of my mouth. You say, "I am rich; I have acquired wealth and do not need a thing." But you do not realize that you are wretched, pitiful, poor, blind and naked. I counsel you to buy from me gold refined in the fire, so you can become rich; and white clothes to wear, so you can cover your shameful nakedness; and salve to put on your eyes, so you can see.

Those whom I love I rebuke and discipline. So be earnest, and repent. Here I am! I stand at the door and knock. If anyone hears my voice and opens the door, I will come in and eat with him, and he with me.

To him who overcomes, I will give the right to sit with me on my throne, just as I overcame and sat down with my Father on his throne. He who has an ear, let him hear what the Spirit says to the churches.

We come now to the last, and worst, of the seven churches of Asia, the opposite to the church of Philadelphia. As nothing about the church of Philadelphia was openly rebuked, so this church is commended for nothing. And yet this was one of the "seven golden lampstands" (1:20). A corrupt church may still be a church. Here we have, as before:

1. The inscription—to whom and from whom:

a. To whom. This letter was written **to the angel of the church in Laodicea** (verse 14). Laodicea was once a famous city, near the river Lycus and surrounded by a vast wall; it boasted three marble theaters and was, like Rome, built on seven hills. It seems that the apostle Paul was instrumental in planting the Gospel in this city. He wrote a letter from Laodicea, which he mentions in his letter to the Colossians: "After this letter has been read to you, see that it is also read in the church of the Laodiceans and that you in turn read the letter from Laodicea" (Colossians 4:16). Paul also sends his greetings to them, as they were not more than twenty miles from Colosse: "Give my greetings to the brothers at Laodicea" (Colossians 4:15). In the fourth century a council was held in Laodicea, but the city has long since been demolished and lies in ruins today. Its ruins are an awe-inspiring monument to the wrath of the Lamb. "They called to the mountains and the rocks, 'Fall on us and hide us from the face of him who sits on the throne and from the wrath of the Lamb!'" (Revelation 6:16).

b. Who sent this message. Here our Lord Jesus calls himself **the Amen, the faithful and true witness, the ruler of God's creation** (verse 15).

(1) **The Amen** is the one who is steady and unchangeable in all his purposes and promises, which are all yes and amen.

(2) He is **the faithful and true witness**, whose testimony of God to people should be received and fully believed, and whose testimony of people to God will be fully believed and taken notice of and will be a swift but true witness against all indifferent, lukewarm people who only pretend to follow Christ.

(3) **The ruler of God's creation.** This may refer either to the first creation, so that Christ is the beginning, that is, the first cause, the Creator, and the Ruler of everything. Or it may refer to the second creation, that is, the church. Christ is the Head of that body, "the firstborn from the dead," as it says in 1:5, from where these titles are taken. Christ, having raised himself up through his own divine power as the Head of a new world, raises up dead souls to be a living temple and church for himself.

2. The contents of the letter, in which we see:

a. The serious charges brought against this church, both its ministers and its people, by One who knew them better than they knew themselves. **I know your deeds, that you are neither cold nor hot. I wish you were either one or the other!** (verse 15). **You are neither cold nor hot.** Worse than that, **I wish you were either one or the other!** Lukewarmness or indifference in religion is the worst attitude in the world. If religion is real, then it is the most wonderful thing; but if it is not real, then it is the worst possible imposture, and we should oppose it strongly. If religion is worth anything, it is worth everything. Indifference in this matter is inexcusable. "Elijah went before the people and said, 'How long will you waver between two opinions? If the LORD is God, follow him; but if Baal is God, follow him'" (1 Kings 18:21). There is no room for neutrality here. Christ expects people to declare themselves openly, either for him or against him.

b. A severe punishment is threatened: **So, because you are lukewarm—neither hot nor cold—I am about to spit you out of my mouth** (verse 16). As lukewarm water turns the stomach and makes one sick, so those who are lukewarm in their profession of Christianity turn Christ's heart against them. He is sick of them and cannot put up with them for long. They may call their lukewarmness charity, meekness, and moderation, but it is nauseous to Christ. They will be finally rejected. For far be it from the holy Jesus to return to what has been rejected.

c. We have one reason for this indifference in religion, and that is self-conceitedness and self-delusion. They thought they were already very well, and therefore they were completely indifferent about becoming better or worse. **You say, "I am rich; I have acquired wealth and do not need a thing." But you do not realize that you are wretched, pitiful, poor, blind and naked** (verse 17). Observe here what a difference there was between the opinion they had of themselves and the opinion Christ had of them.

(1) The good thoughts they had of themselves. **You say, "I am rich; I**

have acquired wealth and do not need a thing." They think they are **rich** and growing richer. They are so **rich** that they have gone beyond the point of wanting to become any richer. Perhaps they had all that their bodies needed, and that made them overlook the necessities of their souls. Or maybe they thought they were well off in their souls. Perhaps they mistook learning for religion. They had wit, and they took it for wisdom. They trusted in ordinances instead of the God of the ordinances. How careful we should be not to mislead our own souls. Doubtless there are many people in hell who once thought they were on the way to heaven. Let us daily beg God that we may not be left to flatter and deceive ourselves over the concerns of our souls.

(2) The contemptible thoughts that Christ had about them. Christ was not mistaken. He knew, though they did not know, that they were **wretched, pitiful, poor, blind and naked.** Their state was indeed a wretched one that called for pity and compassion from others. Though they were proud of themselves, they were pitied by all who knew them.

They were **poor,** though they thought they were **rich.** Their souls were starving in the middle of abundant food. They were greatly indebted to God's justice and had nothing to pay even the smallest part of their debt with.

Further, they were **blind.** They could not see the state they were in, nor their way out of it, nor the danger they were in. They could not see into themselves. They could not see the path ahead. They were blind, and yet they thought they saw. The very light that was in them was darkness; so how great that darkness must have been. They could not see Christ, even though he had been so clearly portrayed and crucified before their eyes. They could not see God by faith, though he was always present in them. They could not look into eternity, though they stood on the brink of it continually.

Again, they were **naked.** They had no clothing for their souls and had neither the garment of justification nor of sanctification. Their nakedness of both guilt and pollution had no covering. They always lay exposed to sin and shame. "All [their] righteous acts [were] like filthy rags" (Isaiah 64:6), which would defile them. They were naked, without house or harbor, and they were without God, who has been the dwelling place of his people in all ages. In him alone can men find rest and safety. The riches of the body will not enrich the soul. The sight of the body will not enlighten the soul. The most convenient house for the body will not provide rest or safety to the soul. The soul is different from the body and must have the accommodation that suits its nature or else in the middle of bodily prosperity it will be wretched and miserable.

d. We have good counsel given by Christ to this sinful people, and that is that they drop the vain and false opinion they had of themselves and endeavor to be what they were in reality. **I counsel you to buy from me** gold refined in the fire, so you can become rich; and white clothes to wear, so you can cover your shameful nakedness; and salve to put on your eyes, so you can see (verse 18). Notice:

(1) Our Lord Jesus Christ continues to give good counsel to those who have ignored his counsels.

(2) The condition of sinners is never desperate as long as they enjoy the gracious calls and counsels of Christ.

(3) Our blessed Lord, the Counselor, always gives the best advice and that which souls are most in need of.

Here, for example, first, Christ counsels them **to buy from me gold refined in the fire, so you can become rich.** Christ tells them where they can find true riches and how they might gain them. They must find them in Christ. Christ does not send them to the steams of Pactolus, nor to the mines of Potosi, but invites people to himself, the Pearl of great price. And how are they to have this true gold from him? They must buy it. That seems to be going against everything that has been said about them. How can the poor buy gold? In the same way that they can buy wine and milk from Christ: "Come, all you who are thirsty, come to the waters; and you who have no money, come, buy and eat! Come, buy wine and milk without money and without cost" (Isaiah 55:1). Something indeed must be parted with, but it is not worldly wealth; we must make room to receive true riches. "Part with sin and self-sufficiency, and come to Christ with a sense of your poverty and emptiness, that you may be filled with his hidden treasure."

Second, these people were **naked.** Christ tells them where they can find clothes to cover the shame of their **nakedness.** This too they must receive from Christ. All they have to do is take off their filthy rags so they can put on the white robes that Christ bought and provided for them. These are Christ's own imputed righteousness for justification and the clothes of holiness and sanctification.

Third, they were **blind. I counsel you to buy from me . . . salve to put on your eyes, so you can see.** They have to give up their own reason and wisdom, which are but blindness to the things of God, and resign themselves to his Word and Spirit. Then their eyes will be opened so they can see their way and know where they are going. Then they will understand their true duty in life. They will then experience a new and glorious scene opening up in their souls. They will have a new world, furnished with the most beautiful and excellent objects. This light is marvelous to those who are being delivered from the powers of darkness. This is the wise and good counsel Christ gives to careless souls. If they follow it, he is bound to make it effective.

e. Here is added a great and gracious encouragement to this sinful people to take the admonition and advice that Christ has given them. **Those whom I love I rebuke and discipline. So be earnest, and repent. Here I** am! I stand at the door and knock. If anyone hears my voice and opens the door, I will go in and eat with him, and he with me (verses 19-20).

(1) This gift was given with true and tender affection. **Those whom I love I rebuke and discipline.** "You may think I have given you hard words and severe rebukes, but it is all out of love. I would not have openly rebuked you in this way and corrected your sinful lukewarmness and vain confidence if I had not been a lover of your souls. Had I hated you, I would have left you alone, to carry on sinning, which would have been your ruin." Sinners ought to take the rebuke of God's Word and his rod of discipline as signs of goodwill for their souls, and should repent and turn to the one who is disciplining them. Better are the frowns and wounds of a friend than the flattering smiles of an enemy. "The kisses of an enemy may be profuse, but faithful are the wounds of a friend" (Proverbs 27:6).

(2) If they would comply with his admonitions, Christ was ready to make them beneficial to their souls. **Here I am! I stand at the door and knock. If anyone hears my voice and opens the door, I will go in and eat with him, and he with me.** Notice here:

First, Christ is graciously pleased by his Word and Spirit to come to the doors of the hearts of sinners. He comes close to them in his mercy and visits them in his kindness.

Second, Christ finds this door closed against him. The heart of man is by nature shut against Christ through ignorance, unbelief, and sinful prejudices.

Third, when Christ finds the heart shut, he does not immediately go away, but he graciously waits.

Fourth, Christ uses all appropriate means to awaken sinners and to encourage them to open the door to him. Christ calls by his Word, and he knocks by the impulses of his Spirit on their consciences.

Fifth, those who open the door to Christ enjoy his presence, to their great comfort and advantage. He will eat with them; he will accept from them what is good. If he finds that what is laid before him is but a poor feast, he will supply what is lacking. He will give fresh supplies of grace and comfort, and so stir up fresh faith and love and delight. In all this, Christ and his repentant people will enjoy pleasant fellowship with each other. Alas, what do careless, obstinate sinners lose by refusing to open the door of the heart to Christ.

3. We now come to the conclusion of this letter. Here, as before:

a. The promise is made to a believer who overcomes.

(1) It is implied here that although this church seemed to be wholly overcome with lukewarmness and self-confidence, yet it was still possible that through the rebukes and counsels of Christ they could be inspired with fresh zeal and vigor and become conquerors in spiritual warfare.

(2) If they did so, all former faults would be forgiven, and they would have a great reward. **To him who overcomes, I will give the right to sit**

with me on my throne, just as I overcame and sat down with my Father on his throne (verse 21). Here it is intimated, first, that Christ himself experienced temptations and conflicts. Second, Christ overcame them all and was more than a conqueror. Third, as the reward of his conflict and victory, he has sat down with God the Father on his throne, with that glory that he had with the Father from eternity, but that he deliberately greatly concealed on earth. He left it, as it were, in the hands of the Father, as a pledge that he would fulfill the work of a Saviour before he reassumed that manifest glory. Having done this, he requests to have his pledge returned, to appear in his divine glory, equal to the Father. Fourth, those who are conformed to Christ in his trials and victories will be like him in his glory. They will sit down with him on his judgment throne at the end of the world, on his throne of glory through all eternity, shining in his beams of light through virtue of their union with him in the mystical body of which he is Head.

b. The letter closes with a general command to pay attention to its message. **He who has an ear, let him hear what the Spirit says to the churches** (verse 22). This reminds everyone who hears this letter read about its contents. This letter is not just meant for individuals and for the rebuke of the church it was sent to, but its message is for all churches of Christ, in all ages, and in all parts of the world. And as there will be similar churches to this one in all succeeding generations, both in their sins and in their graces, they may be sure that God will deal with them as he dealt with the church of Laodicea. This is a pattern that will be followed in all ages. It states what faithful and fruitful churches may expect from God's hand, and what unfaithful churches may expect to suffer at his hand.

Indeed, God's dealings with his churches provide useful instruction for the rest of the world. They must consider all this carefully. "For it is time for judgment to begin with the family of God; and if it begins with us, what will the outcome be for those who do not obey the gospel of God?" (1 Peter 4:17). This concludes Christ's messages to the churches of Asia, the part of the book of Revelation that has letters. We will now move on to the prophetic part of the book of Revelation.

Revelation
Chapter 4

Introduction

In this chapter the prophetic scene opens. As the first part of the book of Revelation contained letters that started with a vision of Christ in chapter 1, so this part of the book of Revelation is introduced with a glorious appearance of the great God. His throne is in heaven, surrounded by the heavenly host. John made this discovery, and in this chapter he records:

1. The heavenly sight he saw (verses 1-7).
2. The heavenly song he heard (verses 8-11).

Verses 1-7

After this I looked, and there before me was a door standing open in heaven. And the voice I had first heard speaking to me like a trumpet said, "Come up here, and I will show you what must take place after this." At once I was in the Spirit, and there before me was a throne in heaven with someone sitting on it. And the one who sat there had the appearance of jasper and carnelian. A rainbow, resembling an emerald, encircled the throne. Surrounding the throne were twenty-four other thrones, and seated on them were twenty-four elders. They were dressed in white and had crowns of gold on their heads. From the throne came flashes of lightning, rumblings and peals of thunder. Before the throne, seven lamps were blazing. These are the seven spirits of God. Also before the throne there was what looked like a sea of glass, clear as crystal.

In the center, around the throne, were four living creatures, and they were covered with eyes, in front and in back. The first living creature was like a lion, the second was like an ox, the third had a face like a man, the fourth was like a flying eagle.

We have here an account of a second vision that the apostle John was privileged to see. **After this I looked, and there before me was a door standing open in heaven.** And the voice I had first heard speaking to me like a trumpet said, "Come up here, and I will show you what must take place after this" (verse 1). **After this**—that is, "not only after I had seen the vision of Christ walking in the middle of the golden lampstands, but after I had taken his messages from his mouth, and had written and sent them to the different churches, as he commanded; after this, I had another vision." Those who benefit from the blessings God has already given them are prepared to receive more, and may expect more. Notice:

1. The preparation made for the apostle receiving this vision.

a. **A door standing open in heaven.** From this we learn:

(1) Whatever happens on earth is first of all planned and settled in heaven. All events are therefore before his eyes, and he allows the inhabitants of heaven to see as much of them as is fit for them.

(2) We can know nothing about the future except what God is pleased to tell us. These events were behind the curtain until God opened the door.

(3) But insofar as God reveals his plans to us, we may and must receive them, and not pretend to be wiser than his revelation.

b. To prepare John for the vision, **the voice I had first heard speaking to me like a trumpet said, "Come up here, and I will show you what must take place after this."** He was called into the third heaven.

(1) There is a way opened into the holiest of all, into which the children of God may enter through faith and holy affections now, in their spirits when they die, and in their complete persons on the last day.

(2) We must not intrude into the secret of God's presence but stay where we are until we are called into it.

c. To prepare for this vision the apostle **was in the Spirit** (verse 2). He was in a rapture, as before: "On the Lord's Day I was in the Spirit, and I heard behind me a loud voice like a trumpet" (1:10). "I know a man in Christ who fourteen years ago was caught up to the third heaven. Whether it was in the body or out of the body I do not know—God knows" (2 Corinthians 12:2). Whether John was "in the body or out of the body," we do not know. Perhaps he himself could not tell. However, all bodily actions and sensations were for a time suspended, and his spirit was possessed with a spirit of prophecy and completely under a divine influence. The more we withdraw from all bodily things, the more we are fit for fellowship with God. We should, as it were, forget the body when we go in before the Lord and be willing to let go of it, so that we may go up to him in heaven. This was the apparatus to the vision. Now observe:

2. The vision itself. It begins with the strange sights that the apostle saw, which were as follows:

a. **There before me was a throne in heaven with someone sitting on it** (verse 2). He saw a **throne** set in **heaven**. This was the seat of honor, judgment, and authority. Heaven is God's throne. There he lives in glory, and from there he gives laws to the church and to the whole world. All earthly thrones are under the jurisdiction of this throne, which is set in heaven.

b. He saw a glorious One on the throne. **And the one who sat there had the appearance of jasper and carnelian** (verse 3). This throne was not empty. The person on it filled it, and he was God. John's description includes the things that are most precious and beautiful in the world. The One on the throne **had the appearance of jasper and carnelian.** He is not described as having any human features, which would depict a certain kind of image; rather, only his transcendent brightness is described. **Jasper** is a transparent stone that nevertheless gives the eye a variety of most vivid colors, signifying the glorious perfections of God. The **carnelian** stone is red, signifying God's justice. This essential attribute he never divests himself of in favor of anyone else, but gloriously uses it as he rules the world, and in particular as he rules the church through our Lord Jesus Christ. This attribute is displayed in pardoning as well as in punishing, in saving sinners as well as in destroying them.

c. **A rainbow, resembling an emerald, encircled the throne** (verse 3). The **rainbow** was the seal and token of the covenant of providence that God made with Noah and his descendants and is a suitable emblem of the covenant of promise that God made with Christ as the Head of the church, and with all his people in him. This covenant is like that concerning the waters of Noah to God—an everlasting covenant ordered in all things, and most certain. This rainbow looked like **an emerald.** The most dominant color was a beautiful green, showing the reviving and refreshing nature of the new covenant.

d. **Surrounding the throne were twenty-four other thrones, and seated on them were twenty-four elders. They were dressed in white and had crowns of gold on their heads** (verse 4). Around the throne John saw **twenty-four other thrones.** These thrones were not empty but were filled with **twenty-four elders.** These **elders,** presbyters, represented, most probably, the whole of God's church, both from the Old Testament and from the New Testament. They were not the ministers of the church but rather the representatives of the people. Their sitting down denotes their honor, rest, and contentment. Their sitting around the throne signifies their relationship to God, their nearness to him, the sight and enjoyment they have of him, and their constant regard for him.

They were dressed in white, denoting that the righteousness of the saints is both imputed and inherent. They **had crowns of gold on their heads,** signifying the honor and authority given to them by God, and the glory they have with him. All this may be applied in a secondary sense to the church in the age of the Gospel here on earth, in its worshiping congregations. In a primary sense it applies to the church triumphant in heaven.

e. **From the throne came flashes of lightning, rumblings and peals of thunder** (verse 5). John saw **lightning** and heard **thunder** coming from the throne. This signifies the awful declarations that God makes to his church about his sovereign will and purpose. He gave the law on Mount Sinai in this way. The Gospel has no less authority and glory than the law, though it does have a more spiritual nature.

f. **Before the throne, seven lamps were blazing. These are the seven spirits of God** (verse 5). The various gifts, graces, and workings of the Spirit of God in Christ's churches are all given according to the will and pleasure of him who sits on the throne.

g. **Also before the throne there was what looked like a sea of glass, clear as crystal** (verse 6). As in the temple, there was a great brass basin filled with water, where the priests went to wash before they ministered before the Lord. This was called a "sea": "He made the Sea of cast metal, circular in shape, measuring ten cubits from rim to rim and five cubits high. It took a line of thirty cubits to measure around it" (2 Chronicles 4:2). So in the church in the age of the Gospel, the sea for purification is the blood of the Lord Jesus Christ, who cleanses us from all sin. Everybody must be washed in this who wants to be admitted into the gracious presence of God on earth or into his glorious presence in heaven.

h. **In the center, around the throne, were four living creatures, and they were covered with eyes, in front and in back** (verse 6). John saw **four living creatures.** They were most probably between the throne and the circle of the elders, standing between God and the people. These seem to signify the ministers of the Gospel, not only because they are nearer to God and between him and the elders or representatives of the Christian people and because there were fewer of them than the people, but because of their description.

(1) By their many eyes. **They were covered with eyes.** This denotes wisdom and vigilance.

(2) By the animals to which they were compared. **The first living creature was like a lion, the second was like an ox, the third had a face like a man, the fourth was like a flying eagle** (verse 7). Note their **lion**-like courage, their great labor and diligence, in which they resemble the **ox,** their prudence and discretion as men, and their sublime affections and speculations by which they could mount up like **a flying eagle.** These wings were full of eyes on the inside (verse 8), showing that in all their meditations and acts of service they acted with knowledge and were especially well acquainted with themselves and the state of their own souls and could see their own concern in the great doctrines and duties of religion as they watched over their own souls as well as over the souls of the people.

(3) By their constant work—that is, praising God, not stopping day or night. The elders sit and are ministered to. But the four living creatures stand and minister; they do not rest day or night. This now leads to the other part of this vision.

Verses 8-11

Each of the four living creatures had six wings and was covered with eyes all around, even under his wings. Day and night they never stop saying:

"Holy, holy, holy is the Lord God Almighty, who was, and is, and is to come."

Whenever the living creatures give glory, honor and thanks to him who sits on the throne and who lives for ever and ever, the twenty-four elders fall down before him who sits on the throne, and worship him who lives for ever and ever. They lay their crowns before the throne and say:

"You are worthy, our Lord and God, to receive glory and honor and power, for you created all things, and by your will they were created and have their being."

We have considered the sights that the apostle saw in heaven. Now let us observe the songs he heard. For there are in heaven not only things to be seen that will greatly please a sanctified eye, but things to be heard that will greatly delight a sanctified ear. This is true also of the church of Christ here, which is a heaven on earth, and it will be eminently true in the church made perfect in the heaven of heavens.

1. He heard the song of the four living creatures, the ministers of the church, which connects with the vision of Isaiah the prophet:

In the year that King Uzziah died, I saw the Lord seated on a throne, high and exalted, and the train of his robe filled the temple. Above him were seraphs, each with six wings: With two wings they covered their faces, with two they covered their feet, and with two they were flying. And they were calling to one another: "Holy, holy, holy is the LORD Almighty; the whole earth is full of his glory."

—Isaiah 6:1-3

Here in the book of Revelation:

a. They adore one God, the one and only, **the Lord God Almighty,** unchangeable and everlasting. **Each of the four living creatures had six wings and was covered with eyes all around, even under his wings. Day and night they never stop saying: "Holy, holy, holy is the Lord God Almighty, who was, and is, and is to come"** (verse 8).

b. They adore three Holies in this one God: the holy Father, the holy Son, and the Holy Spirit. And these are one infinitely holy and eternal Being who sits on the throne and who lives forever (verse 9). In this glory the prophet saw Christ and spoke about him.

2. **Whenever the living creatures give glory, honor and thanks to him who sits on the throne and who lives for ever and ever, the twenty-four elders fall down before him who sits on the throne, and worship him who lives for ever and ever. They lay their crowns before the throne and say . . .** (verses 10-11). John heard the praises of **the twenty-four elders,** that is, of the Christian people represented by them. The ministers led, and the people followed, in the praises of God. Notice here:

a. The object of their worship. This was the same as the ministers adored, namely, **him who sits on the throne,** the eternal, ever-living God. The true church of God has one and the same object of worship. Two different objects of worship would confound the worship and divide the worshipers. It is unlawful to join in divine worship with those who either mistake or multiply the object. There is only one God, and he alone, as God, is worshiped by the church on earth and in heaven.

b. The acts of adoration. First, they **fall down before him who sits on the throne.** They display the most profound humility, reverence, and godly fear. Second, **they lay their crowns before the throne.** They give God the glory of the holiness with which he has crowned their souls on earth, as well as the honor and happiness with which he crowns them in heaven. They owe all their graces and all their glories to him and acknowledge that his crown is infinitely more glorious than their crown, and that it is their glory to be glorifying God.

c. The words of adoration. They said, **"You are worthy, our Lord and God, to receive glory and honor and power, for you created all things, and by your will they were created and have their being"** (verse 11). Notice, first, that they do not say, "We give you glory and honor and power," for what can any creature pretend to give to God? Rather, they say, **"You are worthy, our Lord and God, to receive glory and honor and power."** Second, as they do this, they tacitly acknowledge that God is exalted far above all blessing and praise. He is worthy to receive glory, but we are unworthy to praise and are unable to do this according to his infinite excellencies.

d. The basis and reason for the adoration, which is threefold. First, he is the Creator of all things, the first cause. Nobody except the Creator of all things should be adored. No created thing can be the object of religious worship. Second, he is the Sustainer of all things. Everything that continues to exist does so through his sustaining power. Everything, except for God, is dependent on God's will and power, and no dependent thing should be set up as an object of worship. Part of being a dependent person is to worship, not to be worshiped. Third, God is the final cause of all things. **"By your will they were created."** It was God's will and pleasure to create all things. Nobody made him do this. God made all things at his pleasure, to deal with them as he pleases and to glorify himself in them in one way or another. God does not take pleasure in the death of sinners but wants them to repent and turn to him and live. "The LORD works out everything for his own ends" (Proverbs 16:4).

Now if these things are true and provide sufficient grounds for religious worship, and if they apply exclusively to God, Christ must be God, one with the Father and Spirit, and should be worshiped as such. For we find that what is attributed to the Father is also attributed to the Son. "For by him all things were created: things in heaven and on earth, visible and invisible, whether thrones or powers or rulers or authorities; all things were created by him and for him. He is before all things, and in him all things hold together" (Colossians 1:16-17).

Revelation
Chapter 5

Introduction

In the previous chapter the prophetic stage was set in the sight and hearing of the apostle. He saw God the Creator and Ruler of the world and the great King of the church. He saw God on the throne of glory and government, surrounded by his holy ones and receiving their praises. Now the counsels and decrees of God are set before the apostle as if in a book that God held in his right hand. This book is represented:

1. As sealed in the hand of God (verses 1-5).
2. As taken into the hand of Christ the Redeemer, to be unsealed and opened (verses 6-14).

Verses 1-5

Then I saw in the right hand of him who sat on the throne a scroll with writing on both sides and sealed with seven seals. And I saw a mighty angel proclaiming in a loud voice, "Who is worthy to break the seals and open the scroll?" But no one in heaven or on earth or under the earth could open the scroll or even look inside it. I wept and wept because no one was found who was worthy to open the scroll or look inside. Then one of the elders said to me, "Do not weep! See, the Lion of the tribe of Judah, the Root of David, has triumphed. He is able to open the scroll and its seven seals."

Up to this point the apostle had only seen the great God, Governor of all things. Now:

1. He is favored with a sight of the model and methods of God's rule, as they were written down in a book that he holds in his hand. We are to think of this as shut up and sealed in God's hand. Notice:

a. The designs and methods of divine providence toward the church

61

and the world are stated and fixed. They are written in a book. The great plan is laid out, every part in its place, and it all becomes a matter of record. The original draft of this book is the book of God's decrees, set down in his own cabinet, in his eternal mind. But there is a copy of the parts that need to be known, in the book of Scripture in general, especially in the prophetic books, and in particular in this book of Revelation.

b. **Then I saw in the right hand of him who sat on the throne a scroll with writing on both sides and sealed with seven seals** (verse 1). God holds this book in his **right hand**, thus declaring the authority of the book and his readiness and determination to carry out all of its contents and all the counsel and purposes recorded in it.

c. This book held in God's hand is shut up and sealed. Nobody, apart from God, knows what is in it until he allows it to be opened. "To make plain to everyone the administration of this mystery, which for ages past was kept hidden in God, who created all things" (Ephesians 3:9). But it is his glory to conceal the matter as he pleases. The times and seasons, and the great events, he has kept in his own power and hand.

d. **Sealed with seven seals.** This tells us how secret God's counsels are. They cannot be penetrated by the eye or by the intellect. This also points us to seven different parts of this book of God's counsels. Each part seems to have a particular seal and, when opened, reveals its contents. These seven parts are not unsealed and opened all at once, but one at a time. One scene showing God's providence introduces the next scene, revealing another aspect of divine providence, until the whole mystery of God's counsel and conduct is complete.

2. John heard a proclamation made about this sealed book. **And I saw a mighty angel proclaiming in a loud voice, "Who is worthy to break the seals and open the scroll?"** (verse 2).

a. The voice came from **a mighty angel**, not that there are any weak angels among the angels of heaven, although there are many among the angels of the churches. This angel seemed to call out, not just as a crier, but as a champion, with a challenge to any or all creatures to try in the strength of their wisdom to open the counsels of God. Like a champion, he proclaimed in a loud voice, so all creatures could hear.

b. The cry or challenge proclaimed was: **"Who is worthy to break the seals and open the scroll?"** "If any creature thinks he is capable of explaining or carrying out God's counsels, let him come forward and attempt to do this."

c. Nobody in heaven or earth could accept the challenge or undertake the task. **But no one in heaven or on earth or under the earth could open the scroll or even look inside it** (verse 3). **No one in heaven.** None of the glorious holy angels, even though they are in front of God's throne and are ministers of his providence, could do this. With all their wisdom they were unable to fathom God's decrees. **No one ... on earth.** Not even the wisest and best person could manage this. None of the magicians or soothsayers could help, nor could any of God's prophets say anything more than what God had revealed to them. **No one ... under the earth.** None of the fallen angels, none of the spirits of people who had died, can open this book. Satan himself, with all his subtlety, cannot do it. The creatures cannot open it, nor look at it. They cannot read it; only God can do this.

3. John felt very upset about this. **I wept and wept because no one was found who was worthy to open the scroll or look inside** (verse 4). The apostle **wept,** as this was such a disappointment to him. From what he had seen of him who sat on the throne, he was very keen to know and see more about his mind and will. This desire, when not immediately gratified, filled him with sorrow and brought many tears to his eyes. Notice here:

a. Those who have seen most of God in this world are most desirous to see more. Those who have seen his glory, desire to know his will.

b. Good people may be too eager and too hasty to look into the mysteries of divine conduct.

c. Such desires, not immediately answered, turn to grief and sorrow. Hope deferred makes the heart sick.

4. The apostle was encouraged and comforted to hope that this sealed book would yet be opened. **Then one of the elders said to me, "Do not weep! See, the Lion of the tribe of Judah, the Root of David, has triumphed. He is able to open the scroll and its seven seals"** (verse 5). Notice here:

a. Who it was that gave St. John the hint: **one of the elders.** God had revealed it to his church. If angels do not refuse to learn from the church, ministers should not disdain to do so either.

b. Who it was that would open the scroll—the Lord Jesus Christ. He is called **the Lion of the tribe of Judah,** referring to his human nature. This allusion is from Jacob's prophecy: "You are a lion's cub, O Judah; you return from the prey, my son. Like a lion he crouches and lies down, like a lioness—who dares to rouse him?" (Genesis 49:9). He is also called **the Root of David,** according to his divine nature, even though he was descended from David in his human family tree. He is a "middle" person, God and man, and thus carries out the office of Mediator between God and man and so is worthy of opening and carrying out all God's counsels that apply to men. He does this in his capacity of Mediator, as **the Root of David** and a descendant of Judah. He does this as Head and King of the Israel of God, and he will do it for the consolation and joy of all his people.

Verses 6-14

Then I saw a Lamb, looking as if it had been slain, standing in the center of the throne, encircled by the four living creatures and the elders. He had seven horns and seven eyes, which are the seven spirits of God

sent out into all the earth. He came and took the scroll from the right hand of him who sat on the throne. And when he had taken it, the four living creatures and the twenty-four elders fell down before the Lamb. Each one had a harp and they were holding golden bowls full of incense, which are the prayers of the saints. And they sang a new song:

"You are worthy to take the scroll and to open its seals, because you were slain, and with your blood you purchased men for God from every tribe and language and people and nation. You have made them to be a kingdom and priests to serve our God, and they will reign on the earth."

Then I looked and heard the voice of many angels, numbering thousands upon thousands, and ten thousand times ten thousand. They encircled the throne and the living creatures and the elders. In a loud voice they sang:

"Worthy is the Lamb, who was slain, to receive power and wealth and wisdom and strength and honor and power and praise!"

Then I heard every creature in heaven and on earth and under the earth and on the sea, and all that is in them, singing:

"To him who sits on the throne and to the Lamb be praise and honor and glory and power, for ever and ever."

The four living creatures said, "Amen," and the elders fell down and worshiped.

1. The apostle sees this book taken into the hands of the Lord Jesus Christ, so that he can open it and carry out its commands. Christ is described:

a. By his place and station. **Then I saw a Lamb, looking as if it had been slain, standing in the center of the throne, encircled by the four living creatures and the elders. He had seven horns and seven eyes, which are the seven spirits of God sent out into all the earth** (verse 6). He is **standing in the center of the throne, encircled by the four living creatures and the elders.** He was on the same throne as the Father. He was closer to the Father than any of the elders or ministers of the churches. Christ, as man and Mediator, is subordinate to God the Father, but is nearer to him than all the creatures. "For in Christ all the fullness of the Deity lives in bodily form" (Colossians 2:9). The ministers stand between God and the people. Christ stands as Mediator between God and both ministers and people.

b. The form in which he appeared. Previously he had been called a "Lion" (verse 5); here he appears as **a Lamb**, a Lamb **slain.** He is a Lion to conquer Satan. He is a Lamb to satisfy the justice of God. He appears with the marks of his suffering on him, to show that he intercedes in heaven by virtue of his death. He appears as a Lamb with **seven horns and seven eyes.** He has perfect power to carry out all of God's will. He has perfect wisdom to understand it all and to carry it out in the most effective way.

He has **the seven spirits of God** as he has received the Holy Spirit without measure, in all perfection of light and life and power, by which he is able to teach and rule all parts of the earth.

c. He is described by his actions. **He came and took the scroll from the right hand of him who sat on the throne** (verse 7). He did not take the scroll by violence or by fraud. He managed to do this, as was mentioned in verse 4, because he was **worthy** to do it. He did it because he had the necessary authority and acted under the Father's instructions. God most willingly and justly put the book of his eternal counsels into Christ's hand. And Christ readily and gladly accepted it, for he delights to do and reveal the Father's will.

2. The apostle observes the universal joy and thanksgiving that filled heaven and earth as this transaction took place. No sooner had Christ received this book from the Father's hand than he was worshiped and praised by angels, men, and **every creature** (verse 13). The whole world is full of joy to see that God does not deal with men according to absolute power and strict justice, but by way of grace and mercy through the Redeemer. He governs the world not only as a Creator and Lawgiver, but as our God and Saviour. All the world has reason to rejoice at this.

The song of praise offered up to the Lamb on this occasion is made up of three parts. One part is sung by the church, a second part by the church and the angels, and a third part by **every creature.**

a. The church begins the doxology, as it is more immediately concerned in it. **And when he had taken it, the four living creatures and the twenty-four elders fell down before the Lamb. Each one had a harp and they were holding golden bowls full of incense, which are the prayers of the saints** (verse 8). **The four living creatures** and **the twenty-four elders**, the Christian people under their ministers, led the chorus. Here we observe:

(1) The object of their worship was **the Lamb**, the Lord Jesus Christ. It is God's declared will that "all may honor the Son just as they honor the Father" (John 5:23), for the Son has the same nature as the Father.

(2) Their posture. They **fell down before the Lamb.** They did not worship him in any inferior way but with the most profound adoration.

(3) The instruments used in their praise: **Each one had a harp and they were holding golden bowls full of incense. Harps** were instruments of praise. The **golden bowls** were full of incense, which signify **the prayers of the saints.** Prayer and praise should always go together.

(4) The content of their song was appropriate for the new state of the church, the gospel-state introduced by the Son of God.

First, they acknowledge the infinite suitability and worthiness of the Lord Jesus for this great work of opening and carrying out the counsel and purposes of God. **And they sang a new song: "You are worthy to take the scroll and to open its seals, because you were slain, and with your** blood you purchased men for God from every tribe and language and people and nation" (verse 9). "You are worthy ..." Christ was sufficient for the work and deserved the honor of opening its seals.

Second, they mention the grounds and the reasons for this worthiness. While they do not exclude the dignity of Christ's person as God, without which he would not have been sufficient for the work, yet they mainly insist on the merit of his sufferings that he had endured for them. These made their souls sing for joy and thankfulness. Here, in the first place, they mention his suffering: "Because you were slain, and with your blood you purchased men for God." In the second place they mention the fruits of his suffering. There are two things here: redemption to God and high exaltation. Christ has redeemed his people from their slavery to sin, guilt, and Satan. In this way he has redeemed them to God and set them free to serve him and enjoy him. The high exaltation is mentioned in the following verse: "You have made them to be a kingdom and priests to serve our God, and they will reign on the earth" (verse 10).

Every ransomed slave is not immediately honored. He thinks it favor enough to receive his freedom. But when God's elect were made slaves through sin and Satan, in every nation of the world, Christ not only bought their freedom but bestowed on them the highest honor and preferment. "You have made them to be a kingdom and priests ..." They are to rule over their own spirits and to overcome the world and the evil one. He has made them to be priests and has given them access to himself, and also gave them freedom to offer spiritual sacrifices. "They will reign on the earth," for they will, with Christ, judge the world on the great day.

b. The angels continue the doxology the church had begun. Then I looked and heard the voice of many angels, numbering thousands upon thousands, and ten thousand times ten thousand. They encircled the throne and the living creatures and the elders (verse 11). The angels number thousands upon thousands, ten thousand times ten thousand. They are the attendants around God's throne and guardians of the church. Although they did not need a Saviour themselves, they still rejoice in the redemption and salvation of sinners. They agree with the church in acknowledging the infinite merits of the Lord Jesus when he died for sinners. In a loud voice they sang: "Worthy is the Lamb, who was slain, to receive power and wealth and wisdom and strength and honor and glory and praise!" (verse 12).

(1) He is worthy of that office and authority that requires the greatest power and ... wisdom.

(2) He is worthy of all honor and glory and praise because he is sufficient for the office and is faithful in it.

c. This doxology, begun by the church and taken up by the angels, is echoed by all of creation: Then I heard every creature in heaven and on earth and under the earth and on the sea, and all that is in them, singing: "To him who sits on the throne and to the Lamb be praise and honor and glory and power, for ever and ever" (verse 13). Heaven and earth ring with the praises of the Redeemer. The whole creation benefits from Christ. "He is before all things, and in him all things hold together" (Colossians 1:17). Every creature, had they the understanding and the language, would adore that great Redeemer who delivers them from the slavery under which they groan, through the corruption of men and the just curse pronounced by the great God on fallen mankind. Their song, on behalf of all creation, is a song of **praise and honor.**

(1) **To him who sits on the throne.** They sing to God as God, or to God the Father as the first person of the Trinity, and thus first in the plan of salvation.

(2) **To the Lamb.** They sing to the **Lamb** as the second person in the Godhead and the Mediator of the new covenant. The worship given to **the Lamb** is no different from the worship they give to the Father, for identical **praise and honor** are ascribed to them both. Their essence is the same, but their part in the work of salvation is distinct, and they are worshiped distinctly. We worship and glorify one and the same God for our creation and for our redemption.

The four living creatures said, "Amen," and the elders fell down and worshiped (verse 14). We see how the church that began the heavenly anthem, when heaven and earth join in the concert, concludes everything with their **"Amen."** They end as they began, prostrate before the eternal and everlasting God. Thus we have seen this sealed book passing with great solemnity from the hand of the Creator to the hand of the Redeemer.

Revelation
Chapter 6

Introduction

The book of divine counsels is now in Christ's hand. Christ loses no time but immediately starts to open the seals and reveal the contents. But this is done in such a way that the predictions are very difficult to understand. Up until now the waters of the sanctuary have been like those in Ezekiel's vision, only up to the ankles or knees, or at the most up to the waist. "As the man went eastward with a measuring line in his hand, he measured off a thousand cubits and then led me through water that was ankle-deep. He measured off another thousand cubits and led me through water that was knee-deep. He measured off another thousand and led me through water that was up to the waist" (Ezekiel 47:3-4). Here, however, the waters start as a river that cannot be crossed. The visions that John saw, the letters to the churches, and the songs of praise in the previous chapters and some dark things in them were difficult to understand. Yet they were more like milk for babies than meat for strong men. "You need milk, not solid food! Anyone who lives on milk, being still an infant, is not acquainted with the teaching about righteousness. But solid food is for the mature, who by constant use have trained themselves to distinguish good from evil" (Hebrews 5:12-13).

Now we launch into the deep, and our purpose is not so much to fathom it as to let down our net to take in a load of fish. We will only hint at what seems most obvious. The prophecies of the book are divided into seven seals that have been opened, seven trumpets sounding, and seven bowls poured out. It is supposed that the opening of the seven seals discloses those providences that concerned the church in the first three centuries, from the ascension of our Lord and Saviour to the reign of Constantine. This was represented in a scroll and sealed in several places, so that when one seal was opened you could read part of it, and so on, until the whole of the scroll was revealed. Yet we are not told here what was written in the book, but what John saw in enigmatic figures and hieroglyphics. "It is not for you to know the times or dates the Father has set by his own authority" (Acts 1:7).

In this chapter six of the seven seals are opened, and the visions in them are spoken about:

> The first seal (verses 1-2).
> The second seal (verses 3-4).
> The third seal (verses 5-6).
> The fourth seal (verses 7-8).
> The fifth seal (verses 9-11).
> The sixth seal (verses 12-17).

Verses 1-2

I watched as the Lamb opened the first of the seven seals. Then I heard one of the four living creatures say in a voice like thunder, "Come!" I looked, and there before me was a white horse! Its rider held a bow, and he was given a crown, and he rode out as a conqueror bent on conquest.

Concerning verse 1:

1. Christ, **the Lamb**, opens **the first of the seven seals.** He now starts on the great work of opening and accomplishing the purposes of God for the church and the world.

2. One of the ministers of the church calls on the apostle, with a voice like **thunder**, to come close and observe what then happens.

3. **I looked, and there before me was a white horse! Its rider held a bow, and he was given a crown, and he rode out as a conqueror bent on conquest** (verse 2). Here is the vision itself.

a. The Lord Jesus appears and is riding **a white horse.** White horses are not usually used in war, as they make their riders such an obvious target for the enemy. But our Lord Redeemer was certain about victory and a glorious triumph. He rides on a white horse of a pure but despised Gospel, with great swiftness throughout the world.

b. He **held a bow** in his hand. The convictions left by the Word of God are sharp arrows, and they can reach their target from a distance. Although the ministers of the Word draw the bow at random, God can and will direct it to the joints in the armor. "But someone drew his bow at random and hit the king of Israel between the sections of his armor" (1 Kings 22:34). This **bow**, in the hand of Christ, remains strong and, like Jonathan's, never returns empty. "From the blood of the slain, from the flesh of the mighty, the bow of Jonathan did not turn back, the sword of Saul did not return unsatisfied" (2 Samuel 1:22).

As the rain and the snow come down from heaven, and do not return to it without watering the earth and making it bud and flourish, so that it yields seed for the sower and bread for the eater, so is my word that goes out from my mouth: It will not return to me empty, but will accomplish what I desire and achieve the purpose for which I sent it.

—Isaiah 55:10-11

c. **He was given a crown.** This shows that all who receive the Gospel must receive Christ as King and must be his loyal and obedient subjects. He will be glorified in the success of the Gospel. When Christ was going to war, one would have thought that a helmet would be more appropriate than a **crown.** But he is given a crown as the guarantee and emblem of victory.

d. **He rode out as a conqueror bent on conquest.** So long as the church continues to be militant, Christ will be **a conqueror.** When he has conquered enemies from one age, he meets with new ones in another age. Men go on opposing, and Christ goes on conquering. His historic victories are pledges of future victories. He conquers his enemies in his people also. Their sins are *their* enemies and *his* enemies. When Christ comes with power into their souls, he begins to conquer these enemies, and he goes on conquering in the progressive work of sanctification until he has gained the complete victory. He conquers his enemies in the world as well. Some of these wicked men he brings to worship him; others he makes his footstool.

Observe from this opened seal:

(1) The successful progress of Christ's Gospel in the world is a glorious sight and worth watching. It is the most wonderful and welcome sight that a good man can see in this world.

(2) Whatever convulsions and revolutions happen in the countries and kingdoms of the world, Christ's kingdom will be established and enlarged in spite of all opposition.

(3) A morning of opportunity usually precedes a night of calamity. The Gospel is preached before the plagues arrive.

(4) Christ's work is not done all at once. We like to think that when the Gospel goes out, it should sweep the whole world before it. But it often meets with opposition and moves slowly. However, Christ will do his own work effectively, and in his own time and his own way.

Verses 3-8

When the Lamb opened the second seal, I heard the second living creature say, "Come!" Then another horse came out, a fiery red one. Its rider was given power to take peace from the earth and to make men slay each other. To him was given a large sword.

When the Lamb opened the third seal, I heard the third living creature say, "Come!" I looked, and there before me was a black horse! Its rider was holding a pair of scales in his hand. Then I heard what sounded like a voice among the four living creatures, saying, "A quart of wheat for a day's wages, and three quarts of barley for a day's wages, and do not damage the oil and the wine!"

When the Lamb opened the fourth seal, I heard the fourth living creature say, "Come!" I looked, and there before me was a pale horse! Its rider was named Death, and Hades was following close behind him. They were given power over a fourth of the earth to kill by sword, famine and plague, and by the wild beasts of the earth.

The next three seals give us the sad prospect of great judgments with which God punishes those who either refuse or abuse the everlasting Gospel. While some people understand them to refer to the persecutions that come upon the church of Christ, and others of the destruction of the Jews, they seem more likely to represent God's terrible judgments in general in which he avenges those who make light of his covenant.

1. **When the Lamb opened the second seal, I heard the second living creature say, "Come!"** (verse 3). When the **second seal** was opened, which John was ordered to view, **another horse came out, a fiery red one. Its rider was given power to take peace from the earth and to make men slay each other. To him was given a large sword** (verse 4). This second horse was **a fiery red one.** It is not clear who **its rider** was. It may have been Christ himself, or the Lord of hosts, or the person he raised up to wage this war. But the following is clear:

a. People who will not submit to the bow of the Gospel must expect to be cut down by the **sword** of divine justice.

b. Jesus Christ rules and commands not only the kingdom of grace but also the kingdom of providence.

c. The **sword** of war is a dreadful judgment. It takes away **peace from the earth,** which is one of its greatest blessings, and makes **men slay each other.** People who should love one another and help each other are in a state of war, killing each other.

2. **When the Lamb opened the third seal, I heard the third living creature say, "Come!" I looked, and there before me was a black horse! Its rider was holding a pair of scales in his hand** (verse 5). When the **Lamb opened the third seal,** which John is told to look at, another horse, different from the previous one, appears—a **black horse,** signifying famine and terrible judgment. **Its rider was holding a pair of scales,** signifying that people must eat bread that had been weighed out, as had been threatened: "When I cut off your supply of bread, ten women will be able to bake your supply of bread in one oven, and they will dole out the bread by weight" (Leviticus 26:26). **Then I heard what sounded like a voice among the four living creatures, saying, "A quart of wheat for a day's wages, and three quarts of barley for a day's wages, and do not**

damage the oil and the wine!" (verse 6). The words translated **a voice** in this verse have made some expositors think it was not a vision about famine but about plenty. But if we consider the quantity they weighed out and the value of the money at the time of the prophecy, this objection is removed. They gave a large sum of money for **a quart of wheat.** However, it seems that this famine, like all others, affected the poor most severely. Though **the oil and the wine,** the luxuries of the wealthy, are not damaged, when bread, the staff of life, is sparse, oil and wine cannot take its place. Notice here:

a. When God hates their spiritual food, God may deprive them of their daily bread.

b. One judgment seldom comes on its own. The judgment of war often brings the judgment of famine with it. People who will not humble themselves under one judgment must expect another judgment, and a greater one. For when God fights, he wins. The famine of bread is a terrible judgment, but the famine of the Word is a worse judgment, though careless sinners do not realize this.

3. **When the Lamb opened the fourth seal, I heard the fourth living creature say, "Come!"** (verse 7). John is commanded to watch as **the Lamb opened the fourth seal.** Another horse appears, this time **a pale horse. I looked, and there before me was a pale horse! Its rider was named Death, and Hades was following close behind him. They were given power over a fourth of the earth to kill by sword, famine and plague, and by the wild beasts of the earth** (verse 8). Notice here:

a. The name of the rider. **Its rider was named Death.** Death is the king of terrors. Pestilence, death, reigns over a kingdom or empire. Death on horseback marches about, making fresh conquests every hour.

b. The followers of this king of terrors. **Hades** is a state of eternal misery for all those who die in their sins. During such times of general destruction, multitudes go down unprepared into the valley of destruction. It is awe-inspiring, and enough to make the whole world tremble, to think that eternal damnation follows the death of an impenitent sinner. Observe:

(1) There is a natural as well as a judicial link between one judgment and the other. War is a wasting calamity, and scarcity and famine follow in its wake. And famine, not allowing people proper nourishment and forcing them to eat unwholesome food, brings disease and death in its wake.

(2) God's quiver is full of arrows. He is never at a loss for ways to punish wicked people.

(3) In the book of God's counsels he has prepared judgments for scorners as well as mercy for returning sinners.

(4) In the book of the Scriptures God has openly warned against the wicked as well as given promises for the righteous. It is our duty to observe the threats as well as the promises.

4. After the seals were opened concerning the impending judgments, and a description of them was given, we have this general observation: **They were given power over a fourth of the earth to kill by sword, famine and plague, and by the wild beasts of the earth.** God gave them **power**, that is, instruments of his anger, or those judgments themselves. The One who holds the wind in his hand has all public calamities at his command, and they only end when he banishes them, and they go no further than he permits. To the three great judgments of war, famine, and plague is here added, **the wild beasts of the earth.** This severe divine judgment is mentioned by Ezekiel also: "For this is what the Sovereign LORD says: How much worse will it be when I send against Jerusalem my four dreadful judgments—sword and famine and wild beasts and plague—to kill its men and their animals!" (Ezekiel 14:21). When a country has been ravaged by the sword, famine, and plague, the smallest remnant that exists in the howling desert encourages the **wild beasts** to attack them, and they become an easy prey to them. Other people think **wild beasts** refers to brutish, cruel, savage people who, having divested themselves of all humanity, revel in being the agents of other people's destruction.

Verses 9-17

When the Lamb opened the fifth seal, I saw under the altar the souls of those who had been slain because of the word of God and the testimony they had maintained. They called out in a loud voice, "How long, Sovereign Lord, holy and true, until you judge the inhabitants of the earth and avenge our blood?" Then each of them was given a white robe, and they were told to wait a little longer, until the number of their fellow servants and brothers who were to be killed as they had been was completed.

I watched as he opened the sixth seal. There was a great earthquake. The sun turned black like sackcloth made of goat hair, the whole moon turned blood red, and the stars in the sky fell to earth, as late figs drop from a fig tree when shaken by a strong wind. The sky receded like a scroll, rolling up, and every mountain and island was removed from its place.

Then the kings of the earth, the princes, the generals, the rich, the mighty, and every slave and every free man hid in caves and among the rocks of the mountains. They called to the mountains and the rocks, "Fall on us and hide us from the face of him who sits on the throne and from the wrath of the Lamb! For the great day of their wrath has come, and who can stand?"

In the remaining part of this chapter, the fifth and sixth seals are opened.

1. When the Lamb opened the fifth seal, I saw under the altar the

souls of those who had been slain because of the word of God and the testimony they had maintained (verse 9). As the **fifth seal** is opened, no mention is made of anyone summoning the apostle to observe. This is because either in the previous four seals one of the four living creatures spoke, or because what happened now was kept from the view of present ministers, or because it does not contain any new prophecy about future events but rather opens a spring of support and consolation for those who had been and still were under great tribulation for the sake of Christ and the Gospel. Notice here:

a. The sight that the apostle saw, as the fifth seal was opened, was a most moving sight. **I saw under the altar the souls of those who had been slain because of the word of God and the testimony they had maintained.** John saw the souls of martyrs. Notice here:

(1) Where he saw them: **under the altar**—at the foot of the altar of incense, in the most holy place. He saw them in heaven, at the foot of Christ. So we note, first, that persecutors can only kill the body, and after that they can do nothing more. Souls live on. Second, God has provided a good place in the better world for those who are "faithful, even to the point of death" (2:10) and who are no longer allowed any place on earth. Third, holy martyrs are very close to Christ in heaven. They have the highest place there. Fourth, it is not their own death but Christ's sacrifice that gives them a welcome into heaven and a reward there. They do not wash their robes in their own blood but "in the blood of the Lamb" (7:14).

(2) The reason why they suffered: **the word of God and the testimony they had maintained**—for believing the **word of God** and for attesting to or confessing its truth. This profession of their faith they held on to without wavering, even though they died for it. This is a noble cause—the best that anyone can lay his life down for—faith in God's Word and a confession of that faith.

b. John heard a cry. It was a loud cry and contains a humble explanation about the long delay over avenging justice against their enemies. **They called out in a loud voice, "How long, Sovereign Lord, holy and true, until you judge the inhabitants of the earth and avenge our blood?"** (verse 10). Notice:

(1) Even "the spirits of righteous men made perfect" (Hebrews 12:23) keep a right resentment of the wrong they sustained from their cruel enemies. Even though they die in charity, praying that God would forgive their enemies, just as Christ did, yet they desire the honor of God, Christ, the Gospel, and the conviction of others, and that God will take just revenge on the sin of persecution even while he forgives and saves the persecutors.

(2) They commit their cause to him who takes revenge and leave it in his hand. They do not take vengeance themselves but leave everything to God.

(3) There will be joy in heaven at the destruction of the implacable enemies of Christ and Christianity, as well as over the conversion of sinners. When Babylon falls, it will be said, "Rejoice over her, O heaven! Rejoice, saints and apostles and prophets! God has judged her for the way she treated you" (18:20).

c. He observed the kind reply that was made to this cry: **Then each of them was given a white robe, and they were told to wait a little longer, until the number of their fellow servants and brothers who were to be killed as they had been was completed** (verse 11). This records both what was **given** to them and what was **told** to them.

(1) What was **given** to them: a white robe. This was a robe of victory and honor. Their present happiness was an abundant recompense for their past sufferings.

(2) What was **told** them: that they would be satisfied and at peace within themselves, for it would not be long before **the number of their fellow servants and brothers who were to be killed as they had been was completed.** This language suits the imperfect state of the saints in this world rather than their perfect state in heaven. In heaven there will be no impatience, no uneasiness, and no need for any admonitions. But in this world there is a great need for patience.

Observe, first, that a number of Christians known to God are appointed as sheep for the slaughter, set apart to be God's witnesses. Second, as the measure of the sin of persecutors is filling up, so is the number of the persecuted, martyred servants of Christ. Third, when this number is **completed**, God will take a just and glorious revenge on their cruel persecutors. He will recompense tribulation to those who trouble them, and to those who are troubled, he will give an uninterrupted rest.

2. **I watched as he opened the sixth seal** (verse 12). Some commentators believe this refers to the great revolutions in the Roman Empire in Constantine's time, the downfall of paganism; others, with great probability, to the destruction of Jerusalem, as an emblem of the general judgment and the destruction of the wicked at the end of the world. Indeed, the awful characters of this event are so similar to those signs mentioned by our Saviour as preceding the destruction of Jerusalem that it hardly leaves any room to doubt that the same thing is meant in both places, although some believe that event had already happened. "Immediately after the distress of those days 'the sun will be darkened, and the moon will not give its light; the stars will fall from the sky, and the heavenly bodies will be shaken.' At that time the sign of the Son of Man will appear in the sky, and all the nations of the earth will mourn" (Matthew 24:29-30). Notice here:

a. The tremendous events that were coming. Several occurrences would contribute to make that day and dispensation very dreadful.

(1) **There was a great earthquake. The sun turned black like sack-**

cloth made of goat hair, the whole moon turned blood red (verse 12). There was a great earthquake. This may be taken in a political sense. The very foundations of the Jewish church and state would be terribly shaken, though they seemed to be as stable as the earth itself.

(2) **The sun turned black like sackcloth made of goat hair.** This happened either naturally, by total eclipse, or politically by the fall of the chief rulers and governors of the land.

(3) **The whole moon turned blood red.** The inferior officers, or their military men, would all be wallowing in their own blood.

(4) **The stars in the sky fell to earth, as late figs drop from a fig tree when shaken by a strong wind** (verse 13). **The stars** may signify all the men of note and influence among them, though in lower spheres of activity; there would be a general desolation.

(5) **The sky receded like a scroll, rolling up, and every mountain and island was removed from its place** (verse 14). **The sky** rolled up may mean that their ecclesiastical state would perish and be laid aside forever.

(6) **Every mountain and island was removed from its place.** The destruction of the Jewish nation would affect and frighten all the nations around them, those who were held in highest honor and those who seemed to be most secure. It would be a judgment that would astonish the world.

b. This would lead to a dread and terror that would overwhelm all sorts of people on that great and awful day. **Then the kings of the earth, the princes, the generals, the rich, the mighty, and every slave and every free man hid in caves and among the rocks of the mountains** (verse 15). Neither authority, nor grandeur, nor riches, nor courage, nor strength would be able to come to the aid of people at that time. Indeed, poor slaves, who, one would think, had nothing to fear because they had nothing to lose, would be totally astonished in that day. Notice here:

(1) The degree of their terror and astonishment. It would be so complete that it made them like distracted people. **They called to the mountains and the rocks, "Fall on us and hide us from the face of him who sits on the throne and from the wrath of the Lamb!"** (verse 16). They would be glad to be seen no more, to have no being anymore.

(2) The reason for their terror lay in the anger of **him who sits on the throne.** It lies in **the wrath of the Lamb!** Observe, first, that what displeases Christ also displeases God. They are totally one. What pleases or displeases one, pleases or displeases the other. Second, although God is invisible, he can make the inhabitants of this world aware of his awful frowns. Third, although Christ is a **Lamb,** he can still be angry, and even full of wrath. **The wrath of the Lamb** is exceedingly dreadful, for if the Redeemer, who appeases the wrath of God, is himself our wrathful enemy, where shall we find a friend to plead for us? Those who perish under the wrath of the Redeemer, perish without remedy. Fourth, as men have their

day of opportunity and their seasons of grace, so God has his day of righteous wrath. "**For the great day of their wrath has come, and who can
stand?**" (verse 17). And when that **great day of their wrath has come**, the
most stouthearted sinners will not be able to **stand** before him. All these
terrible events actually happened to the sinners in Judea and Jerusalem on
the day of their destruction, and they will fall on all impenitent sinners at
the general judgment on the last day.

Revelation
Chapter 7

Introduction

The things in this chapter happened after the opening of the six seals, which foretold great calamities in the world. They took place before the sound of the great trumpets, which would give notice of the great corruptions arising in the church. Between these this comforting chapter is inserted. It shows the graces and comforts of the people of God in times of calamity. We have here:

1. An account of the restraint laid upon the winds (verses 1-3).
2. The sealing of God's servants (verses 4-8).
3. The songs of angels and saints on this occasion (verses 9-12).
4. A description of the honor and happiness of those who had faithfully served Christ and suffered for him (verses 13-17).

Verses 1-3

After this I saw four angels standing at the four corners of the earth, holding back the four winds of the earth to prevent any wind from blowing on the land or on the sea or on any tree. Then I saw another angel coming up from the east, having the seal of the living God. He called out in a loud voice to the four angels who had been given power to harm the land and the sea: "Do not harm the land or the sea or the trees until we put a seal on the foreheads of the servants of our God."

After this I saw four angels standing at the four corners of the earth, holding back the four winds of the earth to prevent any wind from blowing on the land or on the sea or on any tree (verse 1). Here we have an account of the restraint laid on the **winds.** By **winds,** I think, is meant those errors and corruptions in religion that would cause a great deal of trouble and mischief to God's church. Sometimes the Holy Spirit is compared with the wind. Here the spirits of error are compared to **the four winds.** Though they are contrary to one another, they also do much harm to the church, God's garden and vineyard, breaking the branches and harming the fruit of the trees. The devil is called "the ruler of the kingdom of the air" (Ephesians 2:2). He, by a great wind, overthrew the house of Job's eldest son. Errors are like winds that shake and carry about the unstable. "Then we will no longer be infants, tossed back and forth by the waves, and blown here and there by every wind of teaching and by the cunning and craftiness of men in their deceitful scheming" (Ephesians 4:14). Notice:

1. They are called the **winds of the earth** because they blow only in the lower parts of the earth. Heaven is always free and clear of them.

2. They are restrained by the ministry of **angels standing at the four corners of the earth.** This indicates that the spirit of error cannot spread unless God allows it. **Angels** minister for the good of the church by restraining its enemies.

3. **Then I saw another angel coming up from the east, having the seal of the living God. He called out in a loud voice to the four angels who had been given power to harm the land and the sea: "Do not harm the land or the sea or the trees until we put a seal on the foreheads of the servants of our God"** (verses 2-3). The restraint of the angels only lasted until **"we put a seal on the foreheads of the servants of our God"** (verse 3). God has special concern and care for his servants in times of temptation and corruption, and he has a way of keeping them safe. First, he establishes them; then he tries them. He has the timing of their trials in his own hand.

Verses 4-8

Then I heard the number of those who were sealed: 144,000 from all the tribes of Israel.

From the tribe of Judah 12,000 were sealed, from the tribe of Reuben 12,000, from the tribe of Gad 12,000, from the tribe of Asher 12,000, from the tribe of Naphtali 12,000, from the tribe of Manasseh 12,000, from the tribe of Simeon 12,000, from the tribe of Levi 12,000, from the tribe of Issachar 12,000, from the tribe of Zebulun 12,000, from the tribe of Joseph 12,000, from the tribe of Benjamin 12,000.

We have here an account of those who were sealed. We see:

1. To whom this work was committed: to an angel, **another angel** (verse 2). While some of the angels were busy restraining Satan and his agents, **another angel** was used to mark out and identify the faithful **servants of our God** (verse 3).

2. How they were to be identified: with **a seal on the foreheads** (verse 3). This **seal** was known to God and was as plain to God as if it appeared

on their foreheads. By this mark they were set apart for mercy and safety in the worst of times.

3. The number of those who were sealed: **Then I heard the number of those who were sealed: 144,000 from all the tribes of Israel** (verse 4). Here we notice:

a. A particular account of those who were sealed from the twelve tribes of Judah. **From the tribe of Judah 12,000 were sealed, from the tribe of Reuben 12,000, from the tribe of Gad 12,000, from the tribe of Asher 12,000, from the tribe of Naphtali 12,000, from the tribe of Manasseh 12,000, from the tribe of Simeon 12,000, from the tribe of Levi 12,000, from the tribe of Issachar 12,000, from the tribe of Zebulun 12,000, from the tribe of Joseph 12,000, from the tribe of Benjamin 12,000** (verses 5-8). Twelve thousand in each tribe were sealed, which adds up to a total of 144,000. In this list the tribe of Dan is left out, perhaps because it was given over so much to idolatry. Also, the order of the tribes is altered, perhaps according to their faithfulness to God.

Some commentators take these to be a select number of the Jews who were reserved for mercy at the destruction of Jerusalem. Others think that time was past, and therefore it is to be more generally applied to God's chosen remnant in the world. If the destruction of Jerusalem had not yet happened, and I think it is hard to prove that it had, it seems better to understand this about the remnant of that people whom God had reserved according to the election of grace. Here we have a definite number of people standing for an indefinite number.

b. A general account of those who were saved out of other nations. **A great multitude that no one could count, from every nation, tribe, people and language** (verse 9). Although the text does not say these people were sealed, yet they were selected by God out of all nations and brought into his church, then stood before the throne. Observe here, first, that God will have a greater harvest of souls among the Gentiles than he had among the Jews. Second, the Lord knows who are his, and he will keep them safe in times of dangerous temptation. Third, although God's church is still a little flock in comparison with the wicked world, it is not a society to be held in contempt but is really large, and will become larger still.

Verses 9-12

After this I looked and there before me was a great multitude that no one could count, from every nation, tribe, people and language, standing before the throne and in front of the Lamb. They were wearing white robes and were holding palm branches in their hands. And they cried out in a loud voice:

"Salvation belongs to our God, who sits on the throne, and to the Lamb."

All the angels were standing around the throne and around the elders and the four living creatures. They fell down on their faces before the throne and worshiped God, saying:

"Amen! Praise and glory and wisdom and thanks and honor and power and strength be to our God for ever and ever. Amen!"

Here we have the songs of saints and angels on this occasion. Notice here:

1. The praises offered by the saints and, it seems to me, by Gentile believers for God's care in reserving so large a remnant of the Jews and saving them from unfaithfulness and destruction. The Jewish church prayed for the Gentiles before their conversion, and the Gentile churches have reason to bless God for his special mercy to so many Jews when the rest were cut off. Notice here:

a. The posture of these praising saints: **standing before the throne and in front of the Lamb,** before the Creator and the Mediator. In acts of religious worship we come close to God and are to think of ourselves as in his special presence. And we must come to God by Christ. The **throne** of God would be inaccessible to sinners were it not for a Mediator.

b. Their dress: they were **wearing white robes and were holding palm branches in their hands.** They were invested with the robes of justification, holiness, and victory. The **palms** made them appear the same as conquerors did in their triumphs. God's faithful servants will make this kind of glorious appearance at the last. "I have fought the good fight, I have finished the race, I have kept the faith. Now there is in store for me the crown of righteousness, which the Lord, the righteous Judge, will award to me on that day" (2 Timothy 4:7-8).

c. Their activity: **they cried out in a loud voice: "Salvation belongs to our God, who sits on the throne, and to the Lamb"** (verse 10). This may be understood either as a hosanna, wishing well to the interest of God and Christ in the church and in the world, or as a hallelujah, giving to God and the Lamb the praise for our great salvation. Both the Father and the Son are linked together in these praises: **to our God . . . and to the Lamb.** The Father planned this salvation, and the Son brought it about. Those who enjoy salvation must and will bless the Lord and **the Lamb.** They will do this publicly and with fitting fervor.

2. In verses 11-12 we see the song of the angels. **All the angels were standing around the throne and around the elders and the four living creatures. They fell down on their faces before the throne and worshiped God, saying: "Amen! Praise and glory and wisdom and thanks and honor and power and strength be to our God for ever and ever. Amen!"** (verses 11-12). Notice here:

a. Where they were: **standing around the throne** (verse 11). They were close to the saints, ready to serve them.

b. Their posture. They were very humble and showed great reverence.

They fell down on their faces before the throne and worshiped God (verse 11). Consider these most excellent of creatures, who never sinned, who were continually before God, falling down on their faces in worship before the Lord! What humility, what profound reverence is appropriate for us vile, frail creatures when we come into God's presence. We should fall down before him. There should be both a reverential spirit and humble behavior in all our comings to God.

c. Their praises. They agreed with the praises of the saints. They added their **Amen** (verse 12) to the saints' praises. In heaven there is perfect harmony between the angels and the saints. Then the angels added more of their own praises: **"Praise and glory and wisdom and thanks and honor and power and strength be to our God for ever and ever. Amen!"** (verse 12). Here, first, they acknowledge the glorious attributes of God—his **wisdom**, his **power**, his **strength**, and so forth. Second, they declare that these divine attributes should be blessed and praised and glorified for all eternity. To this they add their **Amen.** We see in this what the activity in heaven is and will be. We should begin now to tune our hearts for this, to be engrossed in this, and to long for that world where our praises, as well as our happiness, will be perfected.

Verses 13-17

Then one of the elders asked me, "These in white robes—who are they, and where did they come from?"

I answered, "Sir, you know."

And he said, "These are they who have come out of the great tribulation; they have washed their robes and made them white in the blood of the Lamb. Therefore, they are before the throne of God and serve him day and night in his temple; and he who sits on the throne will spread his tent over them. Never again will they hunger; never again will they thirst. The sun will not beat upon them, nor any scorching heat. For the Lamb at the center of the throne will be their shepherd; he will lead them to springs of living water. And God will wipe away every tear from their eyes."

Here we have a description of the honor and happiness of those who have faithfully served the Lord Jesus Christ and suffered for him. Notice here:

1. **Then one of the elders asked me, "These in white robes—who are they, and where did they come from?"** (verse 13). This question was asked by **one of the elders.** This was not for his own information but for John's instruction. Ministers may learn from their people, especially from elderly and experienced Christians. But it is also true that the lowest saint in heaven knows more than the greatest apostle in the world. This question has two parts.

a. **"These in white robes—who are they?"**

b. **"These in white robes . . . where did they come from?"** The question seems to be asked in an admiring way, like in the Song of Songs: "Who is this coming up from the desert like a column of smoke, perfumed with myrrh and incense made from all the spices of the merchant?" (3:6). Faithful Christians deserve our notice and respect. We should take notice of the upright.

2. The answer that the apostle gives tacitly acknowledges his own ignorance and asks this elder for more information. **I answered, "Sir, you know." And he said, "These are they who have come out of the great tribulation; they have washed their robes and made them white in the blood of the Lamb"** (verse 14). John replies, **"Sir, you know."** Those who want to gain knowledge must not be ashamed of their own ignorance, nor despise instruction from any who are able to give it.

3. An account is given to the apostle concerning that noble army of martyrs who stand before God's throne with palms of victory in their hands. Note here:

a. The low and desolate state that they had previously been in. They had **come out of the great tribulation.** They had been persecuted by men, tempted by Satan, and sometimes troubled in their own spirits. They had suffered their possessions being taken away, imprisonment, and even loss of life itself. The path to heaven goes through many tribulations. But no matter how great our tribulation may be, it cannot ever separate us from the love of God. "For I am convinced that neither death nor life, neither angels nor demons, neither the present nor the future, nor any powers, neither height nor depth, nor anything else in all creation, will be able to separate us from the love of God that is in Christ Jesus our Lord" (Romans 8:38-39). Trials, when faced in God's strength, will make heaven more welcome and more glorious.

b. The means by which they had been prepared for the great honor and happiness they now enjoyed. They had **washed their robes and made them white in the blood of the Lamb.** It is not the blood of the martyrs themselves, but the **blood of the Lamb** that washes away sin and makes the soul pure and clean in God's sight. Other blood stains. This is the only blood that makes the **robes** of the saints **white** and clean.

c. The blessedness to which they have now arrived, for which they have been prepared. First, they are happy in their situation. **Therefore, they are before the throne of God and serve him day and night in his temple; and he who sits on the throne will spread his tent over them** (verse 15). They are **before the throne of God,** and God dwells with them—he **will spread his tent over them.** They know that in his presence is fullness of joy. "You have made known to me the path of life; you will fill me with joy in your presence, with eternal pleasures at your right hand" (Psalm 16:11).

Second, they are happy in their work, for they **serve** God continually, and they serve him without weakness or tiredness. Heaven is a state of service, but not of suffering. It is a state of rest, but not of sloth. It is a praising, delightful rest.

Third, they are happy in their freedom from all the unpleasantnesses of this present life. **Never again will they hunger; never again will they thirst. The sun will not beat upon them, nor any scorching heat** (verse 16). In the first place, they lack nothing and feel that they lack nothing. In the second place, they are free from all sickness and pain. They will never be scorched by **the sun** again.

Fourth, they are happy in the love and conduct of the Lord Jesus: **For the Lamb at the center of the throne will be their shepherd; he will lead them to springs of living water** (verse 17). He will feed them and **lead them to springs of living water.** He will give them everything that is pleasant and that refreshes their souls, and so **never again will they hunger** (verse 16).

And God will wipe away every tear from their eyes (verse 18). They are happy because they are delivered from all sorrow and from everything that causes sorrow. **God will wipe away every tear from their eyes.** Previously they had their sorrows and shed many tears, both on account of their sin and their affliction. But **God** himself, with his own gentle and gracious hand, **will wipe away every tear.** These tears will never return. Because they were full of tears, God comes to wipe them away. In this he deals with them like a tender father who finds his much loved child crying. He comforts him, dries his eyes, and turns his sorrow into rejoicing. This should affect the Christian's sorrow in this present world and support him through all his troubles in this life. "He who goes out weeping, carrying seed to sow, will return with songs of joy, carrying sheaves with him" (Psalm 126:6).

Revelation
Chapter 8

Introduction

We have already seen what happened when the sixth seal was opened. We now come to the opening of the seventh seal, which introduced the sounding of the trumpets. A dire scene now opens. Most expositors agree that the seven seals represent the interval between the apostle's time and Constantine's reign. But the seven trumpets are meant to represent the rise of antichrist, some time after the empire became Christian. In this chapter we have:

1. The preface, or prelude, to the sounding of the trumpets (verses 1-6).
2. The sounding of the four trumpets (verses 7-13).

Verses 1-6

When he opened the seventh seal, there was silence in heaven for about half an hour.

And I saw the seven angels who stand before God, and to them were given seven trumpets.

Another angel, who had a golden censer, came and stood at the altar. He was given much incense to offer, with the prayers of all the saints, on the golden altar before the throne. The smoke of the incense, together with the prayers of the saints, went up before God from the angel's hand. Then the angel took the censer, filled it with fire from the altar, and hurled it on the earth; and there came peals of thunder, rumblings, flashes of lightning and an earthquake.

Then the seven angels who had the seven trumpets prepared to sound them.

1. In these verses we have the prelude to the trumpets being sounded, in several parts.

a. **When he opened the seventh seal, there was silence in heaven for about half an hour** (verse 1). **He opened the seventh seal**, the last seal. This introduces a new set of prophetic images and events. The chain of providence continues, one part linked to another, as where one ends, another starts. While they may differ in nature and in time, they all make up one wise, well-connected, and uniform design in God's hand.

b. **There was silence in heaven for about half an hour.** This may be understood to mean:

(1) The silence of peace, for at this time no complaints were heard by the Lord God. All was quiet and well with the church, and therefore all was silent in heaven. For whenever the church on earth cries through oppression, that cry goes up to heaven and resounds there.

(2) Alternatively, this silence may be a silence of expectation. Great things were on the wheel of providence, and God's church, both on earth and in heaven, stood silent, as if waiting to see what God was doing. "Be still before the LORD, all mankind, because he has roused himself from his holy dwelling" (Zechariah 2:13). "Be still, and know that I am God" (Psalm 46:10).

c. **And I saw the seven angels who stand before God, and to them were given seven trumpets** (verse 2). The trumpets were given to the **angels** to **sound them** (verse 6). The angels were still being used as wise and willing instruments of divine providence, and they were given all their materials and instructions from God our Saviour. As the angels of the churches are to sound the trumpet of the Gospel, the angels of heaven are to sound the trumpet of providence, and every one has his part to play.

d. **Another angel, who had a golden censer, came and stood at the altar. He was given much incense to offer, with the prayers of all the saints, on the golden altar before the throne** (verse 3). To prepare for what is to come, **another angel** must first offer **incense.** It is very probable that this other angel is the Lord Jesus, the High Priest of the church, who is here described in his priestly office. He has **a golden censer, much incense,** and total merit in his own glorious person. This **incense** he is **to offer, with the prayers of all the saints, on the golden altar** is his divine nature. Notice:

(1) **All the saints** are praying people. None of God's children are born dumb. "Therefore let everyone who is godly pray to you" (Psalm 32:6).

(2) Times of danger should be praying times, and so should times of great expectation. Both our fears and our hopes should make us turn to prayer. Where the interest of God's church is greatly affected, the hearts of God's people should increase in prayer.

(3) **The prayers of all the saints** themselves need the **incense** and intercession of Christ to make them acceptable and effectual, and there is pro-

vision made by Christ for that purpose. He has his **incense**, his **censer**, and his **altar**. He is himself all that is needed for his people.

(4) **The smoke of the incense, together with the prayers of the saints, went up before God from the angel's hand** (verse 4). The prayers of the saints come up before God with **the smoke of the incense**. No prayer, thus recommended, was ever denied an audience or acceptance.

(5) These prayers, which were accepted in this way in heaven, produced great changes on earth. **Then the angel took the censer, filled it with fire from the altar, and hurled it on the earth; and there came peals of thunder, rumblings, flashes of lightning and an earthquake** (verse 5). The same angel that **took the censer** and offered up the prayers of the saints took that same censer and **filled it with fire from the altar, and hurled it on the earth**. This presently caused strange commotions: **peals of thunder, rumblings, flashes of lightning and an earthquake**. These were the answers God gave to the prayers of the saints and the tokens of his anger against the world, denoting that he would do great things to avenge himself and his people of their enemies. Now all things are ready, and the angels carry out their duty.

Verses 7-13

The first angel sounded his trumpet, and there came hail and fire mixed with blood, and it was hurled down upon the earth. A third of the earth was burned up, a third of the trees were burned up, and all the green grass was burned up.

The second angel sounded his trumpet, and something like a huge mountain, all ablaze, was thrown into the sea. A third of the sea turned into blood, a third of the living creatures in the sea died, and a third of the ships were destroyed.

The third angel sounded his trumpet, and a great star, blazing like a torch, fell from the sky on a third of the rivers and on the springs of water—the name of the star is Wormwood. A third of the waters turned bitter, and many people died from the waters that had become bitter.

The fourth angel sounded his trumpet and a third of the sun was struck, a third of the moon, and a third of the stars, so that a third of them turned dark. A third of the day was without light, and also a third of the night.

As I watched, I heard an eagle that was flying in mid-air call out in a loud voice: "Woe! Woe! Woe to the inhabitants of the earth, because of the trumpet blasts about to be sounded by the other three angels!"

1. Here we read: **The first angel sounded his trumpet, and there came hail and fire mixed with blood, and it was hurled down upon the earth. A third of the earth was burned up, a third of the trees were burned up,**

and all the green grass was burned up (verse 7). **The first angel sounded** the first trumpet, and the events that followed were very dismal. There followed **hail and fire mixed with blood.** Here was a terrible storm. Expositors are not agreed on what it symbolizes. Some say it represents a storm of heresies, a mixture of monstrous errors hitting the church, for in that age Arianism prevailed. Others say it stands for a storm or tempest of war falling on the civil state. Mede takes it to mean the Gothic inundation that broke in on the empire in A.D. 395, the same year that Theodosius died, when the northern nations, under Alaric, king of the Goths, broke in on the western part of the empire. Whatever this storm is, we observe here:

a. It was a very terrible storm—**hail . . . fire . . . blood**—a strange mixture!

b. Its limit. It fell on **a third of the earth . . . a third of the trees** and on **all the green grass,** which was burned up. That is, say some, on a third of the clergy and a third of the laity; others take it to refer to judgment falling on the civil state, on a third of the great men and a third of the ordinary people. Some think it means judgment falling on a third of the Roman Empire itself, which was a third of the then known world. The most severe calamities have their bounds and limits set by the great God.

2. **The second angel sounded his trumpet, and something like a huge mountain, all ablaze, was thrown into the sea. A third of the sea turned into blood** (verse 8). **The second angel sounded his trumpet,** and alarm followed, as in the first, with terrible events. Some people think that this **huge mountain** was the leader or leaders of the heretics. Others, such as Mede, think it refers to the city of Rome, which was sacked by the Goths and Vandals five times within a period of 137 years—first by Alaric in A.D. 410, with great slaughter and cruelty. During these calamities **a third part** of the people, called here **the sea** or collection of waters, was destroyed. **A third of the living creatures in the sea died, and a third of the ships were destroyed** (verse 9). Here the destruction was still limited to the third part, for in the middle of judgment God remembers to be merciful. This storm came crashing in on the maritime and merchant cities and countries of the Roman Empire.

3. **The third angel sounded his trumpet, and a great star, blazing like a torch, fell from the sky on a third of the rivers and on the springs of water** (verse 10). **The third angel sounded his trumpet,** and the alarm had similar effects as before. Some take this to refer to a political star, perhaps an eminent governor, and they then apply it to Augustulus, who was forced to hand over the empire to Odoacer in A.D. 480. Others take it to be an ecclesiastical star, some eminent person in the church, compared to a **blazing . . . torch.** They think it was Pelagius, who proved about this time to be a falling star, and who greatly corrupted the church of Christ. Observe:

a. Where the star fell. **On a third of the rivers and on the springs of water.**

b. What effect it had on them. **The name of the star is Wormwood. A third of the waters turned bitter, and many people died from the waters that had become bitter** (verse 11). It turned those springs and waters into **Wormwood**. So **the waters turned bitter,** and **many people died.** Either the laws, which are the springs of civil liberty and property and safety, were poisoned by arbitrary power, or the doctrines of the Gospel, the springs of spiritual life, refreshment, and vigor to human souls, were so corrupted and embittered by a mixture of dangerous errors that human souls found their ruin where they sought refreshment.

4. **The fourth angel sounded his trumpet, and a third of the sun was struck, a third of the moon, and a third of the stars, so that a third of them turned dark. A third of the day was without light, and also a third of the night** (verse 12). **The fourth angel sounded,** and the alarm was followed by further calamities. Notice:

a. The nature of this calamity. Darkness fell on the great lights of heaven, which give light to the world—**the sun . . . the moon . . . the stars.** These represent either the guides and governors of the church or of the state, who are placed in higher orbits than other people and are to give light and to exercise benign influence upon them.

b. The limitation. It was confined to **a third of** these lights. There was some light both from **the sun** by day and from **the moon and stars** by night, but it was only **a third** of what they had given out before. Rather than determine the answer to the controversies these verses have raised among learned expositors, we choose to make these plain and practical points.

(1) When the Gospel comes to a people and is coldly received and does not properly affect their hearts and lives, it is usually followed with dreadful judgments.

(2) God gives warning to people about his judgments before he sends them. He sounds an alarm through his written Word, through ministers, through people's consciences, and through the signs of the times, so that if people are taken unawares, it is their own fault.

(3) God's anger against his people makes dreadful work among them. It embitters all their comforts and makes even life itself bitter and burdensome.

(4) God does not in this world stir up all his wrath but sets bounds on the most terrible judgments.

(5) Corruption of doctrine and judgment in the church are themselves great judgments and the usual causes and tokens of other judgments coming on a people.

c. Before the other three trumpets are sounded, solemn warning is given to the world: how terrible the calamities would be that would follow, and how miserable those times and places would be on which they fell. **As I watched, I heard an eagle that was flying in mid-air call out in a loud** voice: "Woe! Woe! Woe to the inhabitants of the earth, because of the trumpet blasts about to be sounded by the other three angels!" (verse 13).

(1) The messenger was **an eagle that was flying in mid-air.** It was flying as if it were in a great hurry with an awful message.

(2) The message was a denunciation of further and greater woe and misery than the world had so far endured. There are three woes here, to show how much worse the impending calamities would be than the previous ones, or to hint how every one of the three succeeding trumpets would introduce its particular and distinct calamity. If lesser judgments do not take effect, and the church and the world grow worse under them, they must expect greater judgments. God will be known through his judgments. God expects the inhabitants of the world to tremble when he comes to judge the world.

Revelation
Chapter 9

Introduction

In this chapter we have an account of the sounding of the fifth and sixth trumpets, the appearances that came with them, and the events that would soon follow.

1. The fifth trumpet (verses 1-12).
2. The sixth trumpet (verses 13-21).

Verses 1-12

The fifth angel sounded his trumpet, and I saw a star that had fallen from the sky to the earth. The star was given the key to the shaft of the Abyss. When he opened the Abyss, smoke rose from it like the smoke from a gigantic furnace. The sun and sky were darkened by the smoke from the Abyss. And out of the smoke locusts came down upon the earth and were given power like that of scorpions of the earth. They were told not to harm the grass of the earth or any plant or tree, but only those people who did not have the seal of God on their foreheads. They were not given power to kill them, but only to torture them for five months. And the agony they suffered was like that of the sting of a scorpion when it strikes a man. During those days men will seek death, but will not find it; they will long to die, but death will elude them.

The locusts looked like horses prepared for battle. On their heads they wore something like crowns of gold, and their faces resembled human faces. Their hair was like women's hair, and their teeth were like lions' teeth. They had breastplates like breastplates of iron, and the sound of their wings was like the thundering of many horses and chariots rushing into battle. They had tails and stings like scorpions, and in their tails they had power to torment people for five months. They had as king over them the angel of the Abyss, whose name in Hebrew is Abaddon, and in Greek, Apollyon.

The first woe is past; two other woes are yet to come.

As this trumpet sounded, the things to notice are:

1. **The fifth angel sounded his trumpet, and I saw a star that had fallen from the sky to the earth. The star was given the key to the shaft of the Abyss** (verse 1). **A star that had fallen from the sky to the earth.** Some think this represents some eminent bishop in the Christian church, some angel of the church. Just as pastors are called stars, so the church is called heaven or **the sky.** But expositors fail to agree on who this is. Some think it is Boniface, the third bishop of Rome, who assumed the title of universal bishop through the favor of Emperor Phocas, who, being a usurper and tyrant in the state, allowed Boniface to be such a person in the church as the reward for his flattery.

2. **The star was given the key to the shaft of the Abyss.** Having now ceased from being Christ's minister, he becomes the antichrist, the minister of the devil. By Christ's permission, who had taken from him the keys of the church, he becomes the devil's turnkey and lets loose the powers of hell against Christ's churches.

3. **When he opened the Abyss, smoke rose from it like the smoke from a gigantic furnace. The sun and sky were darkened by the smoke from the Abyss** (verse 2). The devil's armies are the powers of darkness, and hell is the place of darkness. The devil carries on his designs by blinding the eyes of men—extinguishing light and knowledge and promoting ignorance and error. He starts by deceiving people and ends by destroying them. Wretched souls follow him in the dark, or they would not dare to follow him.

4. **And out of the smoke locusts came down upon the earth and were given power like that of scorpions of the earth** (verse 3). **Locusts** came out of this **smoke.** Locusts, one of the plagues of Egypt, the devil's emissaries headed by antichrist, all the rabble of anti-Christian orders, promote superstition, idolatry, error, and cruelty. **They were told not to harm the grass of the earth or any plant or tree, but only those people who did not have the seal of God on their foreheads** (verse 4).The locusts had, by God's permission, power to hurt those who did not have God's **seal on their foreheads.**

5. The harm they were able to inflict was not physical but spiritual. They did not kill everyone with fire and sword as in a military battle. They left the **grass** and plants and trees untouched. **They were not given power to kill them, but only to torture them for five months. And the agony they suffered was like that of the sting of a scorpion when it strikes a man** (verse 5). Those they hurt, they did not kill. **They were not given power to kill.** They would not inflict persecution but a secret poison and infection in men's souls that would rob them of their purity and after-

wards their peace. Heresy is a poison in the soul, working slowly and secretly, but it will be bitter in the end.

6. They had no power to hurt those who had God's seal on their foreheads. God's electing, effectual, distinguishing grace will preserve his people from total and final apostasy.

7. The power given to work evil is limited in time to **five months.** This is a definite period of time, a short period of time, though how short we cannot tell. Gospel-seasons have their limits, and times of seduction are limited too.

8. Though it would be short, it would be very sharp, insomuch that those who were made to feel the malignity of the poison in their consciences would be weary of their lives. **During those days men will seek death, but will not find it; they will long to die, but death will elude them** (verse 6). Who can bear a wounded spirit?

9. **The locusts looked like horses prepared for battle. On their heads they wore something like crowns of gold, and their faces resembled human faces** (verse 7). These **locusts** were monstrous in size and shape. They were equipped for their work **like horses prepared for battle.**

a. They pretended to have great authority and seemed to be certain of victory. **They wore something like crowns of gold.** But it was a counterfeit authority.

b. They had the trappings of wisdom. **Their faces resembled human faces,** but they had the spirits of the devil.

c. They had all the allurements of beauty, in order to trap and defile people's minds. **Their hair was like women's hair, and their teeth were like lions' teeth** (verse 8). **Their hair was like women's hair.** That is, their worship was very gaudy and ornamental.

d. While they appeared to have the tenderness of women, **their teeth were like lions' teeth.** In reality they were cruel creatures.

e. **They had breastplates like breastplates of iron, and the sound of their wings was like the thundering of many horses and chariots rushing into battle** (verse 9). They had the defense and protection of earthly powers, **breastplates of iron.**

f. They made a great noise in the world. They flew about from one country to another, making the noise like an army of **many horses and chariots rushing into battle.**

g. **They had tails and stings like scorpions, and in their tails they had power to torment people for five months** (verse 10). Although at first they soothed and flattered people by their fine appearance, they had a sting in their tails. The cup of their abominations contained that which, though delightful at first, would later sting like a scorpion and bite like an adder.

h. The king and commander of this hellish squadron is described here:

(1) **They had as king over them the angel of the Abyss, whose name**

in Hebrew is Abaddon, and in Greek, Apollyon (verse 11). By nature he was an **angel**, and he had once lived in heaven.

(2) **The angel of the Abyss.** He was still an angel but a fallen angel, fallen into **the Abyss,** the bottomless pit, so deep that it was impossible to return from it.

(3) In these infernal regions he is a prince or governor and has the powers of darkness under his rule and command.

(4) His true name is **Abbadon . . . Apollyon,** "destroyer," for destruction is his business and his purpose. He is very successful in this and takes great delight in it. As part of his destroying work, he sends out his emissaries and armies to destroy people's souls. **The first woe is past; two other woes are yet to come** (verse 12). We have here the end of one woe; and where one ends, another begins.

Verses 13-21

The sixth angel blew his trumpet, and I heard a voice coming from the horns of the golden altar that is before God. It said to the sixth angel who had the trumpet, "Release the four angels who are bound at the great river Euphrates." And the four angels who had been kept ready for this very hour and day and month and year were released to kill a third of mankind. The number of the mounted troops was two hundred million. I heard their number.

The horses and riders I saw in my vision looked like this: Their breastplates were fiery red, dark blue, and yellow as sulfur. The heads of the horses resembled the heads of lions, and out of their mouths came fire, smoke and sulfur. A third of mankind was killed by the three plagues of fire, smoke and sulfur that came out of their mouths. The power of the horses was in their mouths and in their tails; for their tails were like snakes, having heads with which they inflict injury.

The rest of mankind that were not killed by these plagues still did not repent of the work of their hands; they did not stop worshiping demons, and idols of gold, silver, bronze, stone and wood—idols that cannot see or hear or walk. Nor did they repent of their murders, their magic arts, their sexual immorality or their thefts.

Here let us consider the preface to this vision, and then the vision itself.

1. The preface to this vision. **The sixth angel blew his trumpet, and I heard a voice coming from the horns of the golden altar that is before God** (verse 13). **A voice** came **from the horns of the golden altar.** Here we note:

a. The power of the church's enemies is restrained until God gives the word to have them turned loose.

b. When nations are ripe for punishment, those instruments of God's anger that had previously been restrained are let loose on them. **It said to** the sixth angel who had the trumpet, "Release the four angels who are bound at the great river Euphrates" (verse 14).

c. The instruments that God makes use of to punish a people may sometimes be far away from them, so that they do not appear to be dangerous at all. These four messengers of God's judgment were **bound at the great river Euphrates,** far away from the European nations. This is where the empire of Turkey grew, which seems to be the subject of this vision.

2. The vision itself. **And the four angels who had been kept ready for this very hour and day and month and year were released to kill a third of mankind** (verse 15). **The four angels** who had been bound are now **released.** Notice here:

a. The length of their military operations is limited to an hour and a day and a month and a year. We find it difficult to interpret prophecies about time. But in general the time is fixed to an hour, to a time when it will start and when it will end. Its extent is also limited, to **a third of mankind.** God will turn the wrath of man to his praise, and the rest of his wrath he will restrain.

b. The army that will execute this great commission is mustered. **The number of the mounted troops was two hundred million. I heard their number** (verse 16). The horsemen number **two hundred million.** We are left to guess how many infantry there literally were. In general, this tells us that the armies of the Muslim Empire would be vast, and this was certainly true.

c. Their formidable equipment and appearance. **The horses and riders I saw in my vision looked like this: Their breastplates were fiery red, dark blue, and yellow as sulfur. The heads of the horses resembled the heads of lions, and out of their mouths came fire, smoke and sulfur** (verse 17). As the horses were fierce, like lions, and eager to rush into battle, so those who sat on them were dressed in bright and expensive armor, with all the emblems of military courage, zeal, and resolution.

d. The vast havoc and desolation they made in the Roman Empire, which had now become anti-Christian. A third of them were killed. They went as far as their commission allowed them, and they could go no further.

e. Their artillery. **A third of mankind was killed by the three plagues of fire, smoke and sulfur that came out of their mouths** (verse 18). With their artillery they made a terrible slaughter, described as **plagues of fire, smoke and sulfur** coming out of the **mouths** of their horses. **The power of the horses was in their mouths and in their tails; for their tails were like snakes, having heads with which they inflict injury** (verse 19). The destruction was also made through the stings in their tails. Mede thinks that this is a prediction of great guns, those cruel instruments that cause such destruction. He observes that these were first used by the Turks at the siege of Constantinople and, being new and strange, were very terrible and caused terrible fatalities. However, there seems to be an allusion to what is mentioned in the former vision, namely, that as antichrist had his forces of a spiritual nature, like scorpions poisoning people's minds with error and idolatry, so the Turks, who were raised up to punish the anti-Christian apostasy, had their scorpions and their stings too, to hurt and kill the bodies of those who had been the murderers of so many souls.

f. Lastly, note the impenitence of the anti-Christian generation under these dreadful judgments. **The rest of mankind that were not killed by these plagues still did not repent of the work of their hands; they did not stop worshiping demons, and idols of gold, silver, bronze, stone and wood—idols that cannot see or hear or walk** (verse 20). The rest of the men who were not killed did not repent. They persisted in those sins for which God was punishing them. These sins were:

(1) Their idolatry. They would not throw out their images, even though they were useless since they could not **see or hear or walk.**

(2) Their murders. **Nor did they repent of their murders** (verse 21). They had killed Christ's saints and servants.

(3) Their sorceries. They had their **magic arts**, rites of exorcism and other things.

(4) Their **sexual immorality.** They allowed both spiritual and physical impurity and promoted it in themselves and others.

(5) Their **thefts.** Through unjust means they accumulated great wealth, at the expense of families, cities, princes, and nations. These are the flagrant crimes of antichrist and his agents. Even though God had revealed his wrath from heaven against them, they are obstinate, hardened, and impenitent, and so must be destroyed.

From this sixth trumpet we learn, first, that God can make one enemy of the church to be a scourge and plague to another. Second, the Lord of hosts has vast armies at his command, to serve his own purposes. Third, the most formidable powers are bounded by limits they cannot go beyond. Fourth, when God's judgments are on the earth, he expects people to repent of their sin and learn righteousness. Fifth, being unrepentant under divine judgment is a sin that will ruin sinners; for where God judges, he will overcome.

Revelation
Chapter 10

Introduction

This chapter is an introduction to the latter part of the prophecies of this book. Whether what comes between this and the sounding of the seventh trumpet (11:15) is a separate prophecy from the other or only a more general account of some of the principal things included in the other is disputed by curious inquirers into these abstruse writings. However, we have here:

1. A remarkable description of a very glorious angel with an open book in his hand (verses 1-3).
2. An account of seven thunders that the apostle heard, echoing the voice of this angel and communicating some discoveries about which the apostle was not yet allowed to write (verse 4).
3. The solemn oath taken by him who had the book in his hand (verses 5-7).
4. The charge given to the apostle and observed by him (verses 8-11).

Verses 1-7

Then I saw another mighty angel coming down from heaven. He was robed in a cloud, with a rainbow above his head; his face was like the sun, and his legs were like fiery pillars. He was holding a little scroll, which lay open in his hand. He planted his right foot on the sea and his left foot on the land, and he gave a loud shout like the roar of a lion. When he shouted, the voices of the seven thunders spoke. And when the seven thunders spoke, I was about to write; but I heard a voice from heaven say, "Seal up what the seven thunders have said and do not write it down."

Then the angel I had seen standing on the sea and on the land raised his right hand to heaven. And he swore by him who lives for ever and ever, who created the heavens and all that is in them, the earth and all that is in it, and the sea and all that is in it, and said, "There will be no more delay! But in the days when the seventh angel is about to sound his trumpet, the mystery of God will be accomplished, just as he announced to his servants the prophets."

Here we have an account of another vision the apostle was favored with, between the sounding of the sixth and seventh trumpets.

1. The person who was principally concerned in communicating this discovery to John was an angel from heaven. **Then I saw another mighty angel coming down from heaven. He was robed in a cloud, with a rainbow above his head; his face was like the sun, and his legs were like fiery pillars** (verse 1). **Then I saw another mighty angel.** This angel is depicted in such a way that we conclude it could be no other than our Lord and Saviour Jesus Christ.

a. **He was robed in a cloud.** He veils his glory, which is too great for mortals to view. "He made darkness his canopy around him—the dark rain clouds of the sky" (2 Samuel 22:12).

b. **A rainbow above his head.** He always keeps his covenant in mind. When his behavior is most mysterious, it remains perfectly just and faithful.

c. **His face was like the sun.** His face was all bright, and full of luster and majesty. "His face was like the sun shining in all its brilliance" (1:16).

d. **His legs were like fiery pillars.** All his ways, both of grace and providence, are pure and steady.

2. His station and posture. **He was holding a little scroll, which lay open in his hand. He planted his right foot on the sea and his left foot on the land** (verse 2), showing the absolute power and dominion he had over the world. **He was holding a little scroll, which lay open in his hand.** This is probably the same scroll that had previously been sealed but was now opened and was gradually fulfilled by him.

3. His voice was awe-inspiring. **And he gave a loud shout like the roar of a lion. When he shouted, the voices of the seven thunders spoke** (verse 3). His awe-inspiring voice was echoed by **the seven thunders,** solemn and terrible ways of discovering God's mind.

4. The prohibition given to the apostle: that he should not make this known but rather conceal what he had learned. **And when the seven thunders spoke, I was about to write; but I heard a voice from heaven say, "Seal up what the seven thunders have said and do not write it down"** (verse 4). The apostle wanted to record and make known everything he saw and heard in these visions, but it was not the time to do this.

5. The solemn oath taken by this mighty angel. **Then the angel I had seen standing on the sea and on the land raised his right hand to heaven** (verse 6).

a. The type of oath he took. **And he swore by him who lives for ever and ever, who created the heavens and all that is in them, the earth and all that is in it, and the sea and all that is in it, and said, "There will be no more delay!"** (verse 6). He raised his right hand to heaven. **And he swore by him who lives for ever and ever** (verses 5-6). He swore by God himself, as God has often done; or by God as God, to whom he, as Lord, Redeemer, and Ruler of the world, now appeals.

b. The content of the oath. **"There will be no more delay!"** This may mean there will be no more delay in fulfilling the predictions of this book, rather than referring to the last angel's sounding. Then everything would be speedily fulfilled. **But in the days when the seventh angel is about to sound his trumpet, the mystery of God will be accomplished, just as he announced to his servants the prophets** (verse 7). **"The mystery of God will be accomplished."** Or this may mean that when this **mystery of God** is ended, time itself will be no more, as it measures the things that are prone to change. Then all things will be forever fixed, and time itself swallowed up in eternity.

Verses 8-11

Then the voice that I had heard from heaven spoke to me once more: "Go, take the scroll that lies open in the hand of the angel who is standing on the sea and on the land."

So I went to the angel and asked him to give me the little scroll. He said to me, "Take it and eat it. It will turn your stomach sour, but in your mouth it will be as sweet as honey." I took the little scroll from the angel's hand and ate it. It tasted as sweet as honey in my mouth, but when I had eaten it, my stomach turned sour. Then I was told, "You must prophesy again about many peoples, nations, languages and kings."

Here we have:

1. A strict order given to the apostle, which was:

a. **"Go, take the scroll that lies open in the hand of the angel who is standing on the sea and on the land"** (verse 8). He was to take the scroll from the hands of the mighty angel previously mentioned. This order was not given by the angel himself who stood on the earth, but by **the voice that I had heard from heaven,** which in verse 4 had ordered him not to write down what he had learned from **the seven thunders.**

b. **So I went to the angel and asked him to give me the little scroll. He said to me, "Take it and eat it. It will turn your stomach sour, but in your mouth it will be as sweet as honey"** (verse 9). This part of the order was given by the angel himself, hinting to the apostle that before he should make known what he discovered, he must more thoroughly digest the predictions and be himself suitably affected with them.

2. An account of the taste of the little book, when the apostle had eaten it. **I took the little scroll from the angel's hand and ate it. It tasted as sweet as honey in my mouth, but when I had eaten it, my stomach turned sour** (verse 10). At first **it tasted as sweet as honey in my mouth.** Everyone enjoys looking into the future and hearing the future foretold. All good people love to hear a word from God, whatever it may say. But when the apostle had digested this book of prophecy more fully, the contents became more bitter. **When I had eaten it, my stomach turned sour.** These things—the grievous persecutions of God's people and the desolations made in the earth—were so terrible that foreknowledge about them would not be pleasant. Rather, this foresight troubled the mind of the apostle. Ezekiel had prophesied in a similar way: "Then he said to me, 'Son of man, eat this scroll I am giving you and fill your stomach with it.' So I ate it, and it tasted as sweet as honey in my mouth" (Ezekiel 3:3).

3. The apostle carries out the orders he was given. **I took the little scroll from the angel's hand and ate it.** He found that it had a sweet taste in his mouth, as he had been told that it would.

a. God's servants should digest in their souls the messages they bring to others in his name and be suitably affected by them themselves.

b. God's servants should deliver every message they are given, whether the messages please or displease people. The messages they like least may be the most profitable ones. God's messengers must not keep back any part of God's counsels.

4. The apostle is told that this book of prophecy that he had now eaten was not given just to gratify his curiosity or to give him pleasure or pain, but was to be relayed through him to the world. Here his prophetic commission is renewed, and he is ordered to prepare for another mission, to convey those declarations about God's mind and will that are of such importance to the whole world. **Then I was told, "You must prophesy again about many peoples, nations, languages and kings"** (verse 11). This message was for **many peoples, nations, languages and kings**, including the greatest people on earth. The messages would be recorded in many **languages.** This is indeed the case. We have them in our own language, and we are obliged to listen to them and to humbly find out what they mean and to believe firmly that everything will be fulfilled at its correct time. And when the prophecies are fulfilled, the meaning and truth of them will be seen, and the continual presence, power, and faithfulness of the great God will be adored.

Revelation
Chapter 11

Introduction

In this chapter we have an account of:

1. The measuring rod given to the apostle, so he could measure the temple (verses 1-2).
2. God's two witnesses (verses 3-14).
3. The sounding of the seventh trumpet and what followed (verses 15-19).

Verses 1-2

I was given a reed like a measuring rod and was told, "Go and measure the temple of God and the altar, and count the worshipers there. But exclude the outer court; do not measure it, because it has been given to the Gentiles. They will trample on the holy city for 42 months."

This prophetic message about measuring the temple is a clear reference to what we find in Ezekiel's vision:

> *I saw a man whose appearance was like bronze; he was standing in the gateway with a linen cord and a measuring rod in his hand. The man said to me, "Son of man, look with your eyes and hear with your ears and pay attention to everything I am going to show you, for that is why you have been brought here. Tell the house of Israel everything you see."*
>
> *I saw a wall completely surrounding the temple area. The length of the measuring rod in the man's hand was six long cubits, each of which was a cubit and a handbreadth. He measured the wall; it was one measuring rod thick and one rod high.*
>
> —Ezekiel 40:3-5; see also Ezekiel 40:6—41:26

But it is not easy to understand either vision—in Revelation or in Ezekiel. It would seem that the purpose of measuring the temple in Ezekiel's vision was so the temple could be rebuilt, which would clearly be beneficial. The purpose of the measuring in John's vision could be one of three things. First, it could be to preserve it in those dangerous times that are foretold. Second, it could be to test it, to see how far it matches up with the standard and pattern on the mount. Third, it could be to reform it, so that what is redundant could be discarded, and what is left could be molded to the true model. Notice:

1. How much was to be measured. **I was given a reed like a measuring rod and was told, "Go and measure the temple of God and the altar, and count the worshipers there"** (verse 1).

a. **"Measure the temple."** The church in general should be built and constituted as gospel-rule directs—whether it is too narrow or too large, or whether the door is too wide or too narrow.

b. **"Measure . . . the altar."** The altar was the place where the most solemn acts of worship were carried out and may represent all religious worship in general. The true altar of the church is Christ, before whom people must bring and lay down all their offerings. The correct way to worship at this **altar** is to worship Christ in spirit and in truth. "A time is coming and has now come when the true worshipers will worship the Father in spirit and truth, for they are the kind of worshipers the Father seeks. God is spirit, and his worshipers must worship in spirit and in truth" (John 4:23-24).

c. **The worshipers** too must be measured. It must be seen if they are making God's glory their purpose and his Word their rule in all their worship. It must be seen if they come to worship God in the right frame of mind, and whether their lives are lived in line with the Gospel.

2. What is not measured and why it is not measured. **"But exclude the outer court; do not measure it, because it has been given to the Gentiles. They will trample on the holy city for 42 months"** (verse 2).

a. What was not to be measured: **exclude the outer court.** Some commentators say that Herod, in the additions he made to the temple, built an outer court and called it the court of the Gentiles. Some people tell us that Hadrian built the city and the outer court, called it Aelia, and gave it to the Gentiles.

b. Why was **the outer court** not to be measured? It was not part of the temple, according to the model either of Solomon or Zerubbabel, and therefore God would not mention it. He would not earmark it for preservation. As it was designed for the Gentiles, to bring pagan ceremonies and customs and annex them to the gospel-churches, so Christ abandoned it to them, to be used as they pleased. Both the court of the Gentiles and the city **they will trample on** will be trodden underfoot **for 42 months.** Some people think this refers to the whole reign of the antichrist. Those who worship in the outer court are either those who worship in a false way or with hypocritical hearts. God rejects such people, who will be found to be his enemies. From all of this we see:

(1) God will have a temple and an altar in the world until the end of time.

(2) He has a strict eye on this temple and notices everything that goes on there.

(3) Those who worship in the outer court will be rejected, and only those who worship behind the curtain are accepted. "We have this hope as an anchor for the soul, firm and secure. It enters the inner sanctuary behind the curtain, where Jesus, who went before us, has entered on our behalf" (Hebrews 6:19-20).

(4) **The holy city**, the visible church, is often trodden on in the world.

(5) But the desolations of the church are for a limited time, a short time, and she will be delivered from all her troubles.

Verses 3-13

"And I will give power to my two witnesses, and they will prophesy for 1,260 days, clothed in sackcloth." These are the two olive trees and the two lampstands that stand before the Lord of the earth. If anyone tries to harm them, fire comes from their mouths and devours their enemies. This is how anyone who wants to harm them must die. These men have power to shut up the sky so that it will not rain during the time they are prophesying; and they have power to turn the waters into blood and to strike the earth with every kind of plague as often as they want.

Now when they have finished their testimony, the beast that comes up from the Abyss will attack them, and overpower and kill them. Their bodies will lie in the street of the great city, which is figuratively called Sodom and Egypt, where also their Lord was crucified. For three and a half days men from every people, tribe, language and nation will gaze on their bodies and refuse them burial. The inhabitants of the earth will gloat over them and will celebrate by sending each other gifts, because these two prophets had tormented those who live on the earth.

But after the three and a half days a breath of life from God entered them, and they stood on their feet, and terror struck those who saw them. Then they heard a loud voice from heaven saying to them, "Come up here." And they went up to heaven in a cloud, while their enemies looked on.

At that very hour there was a severe earthquake and a tenth of the city collapsed. Seven thousand people were killed in the earthquake, and the survivors were terrified and gave glory to the God of heaven.

In this time of treading down, God has reserved for him his faithful

witnesses, who will not fail to attest to the truth of his Word and worship and the excellency of his ways. Notice here:

1. The number of these witnesses. **"And I will give power to my two witnesses, and they will prophesy for 1,260 days, clothed in sackcloth"** (verse 3). It is only a small number, but it is enough.

a. One witness, when Christ's cause is on trial, is worth many at other times.

b. It is a sufficient number, for in the mouth of two witnesses every cause will be established. Christ sent out his disciples two by two to preach the Gospel. Some people think these **two witnesses** are Moses and Elijah, who are to return to the earth for a time. Others think this refers to the church of the believing Jews and of the Gentiles. It would rather appear they are God's eminent faithful ministers who will not only continue to profess the Christian religion but to preach it in the worst of times.

2. The time of their prophesying or bearing their testimony for Christ. **They will prophesy for 1,260 days.** Many people think this refers to the reign of antichrist. If the beginning of that interval could be ascertained, this number of prophetic days, taking a day as a year, would tell us when the end will be.

3. Their dress and posture. They prophesy **clothed in sackcloth,** as those who are deeply affected with the low and distressed state of the churches and lack of interest toward Christ in the world.

4. How they were supported while they carried out their great and hard work. **These are the two olive trees and the two lampstands that stand before the Lord of the earth** (verse 4). They stood before the God of the whole earth, and he gave them the power to prophesy. He made them to be like Zerubbabel and Joshua. The **two olive trees and the two lampstands** are seen in Zechariah's vision: "Then the angel who talked with me returned and wakened me, as a man is wakened from his sleep. He asked me, 'What do you see?' I answered, 'I see a solid gold lampstand with a bowl at the top and seven lights on it, with seven channels to the lights. Also there are two olive trees by it, one on the right of the bowl and the other on the left'" (Zechariah 4:1-3). God gave them the oil of holy zeal and courage and strength and comfort. He made them **olive trees,** and their lamps of profession were kept burning by the oil of inner gracious principles that they received from God. They had oil not only in their lamps but in themselves. Their spiritual life was full of light and zeal.

5. Their security and defense during the time of their prophesying. **If anyone tries to harm them, fire comes from their mouths and devours their enemies. This is how anyone who wants to harm them must die** (verse 5). Some people think this alludes to Elijah calling fire from heaven to consume the captains and groups of men that came to capture him. "'If I am a man of God,' Elijah replied, 'may fire come down from heaven and consume you and your fifty men!' Then the fire of God fell from heaven

and consumed him and his fifty men" (2 Kings 1:12). God promised the prophet Jeremiah, "Because the people have spoken these words, I will make my words in your mouth a fire and these people the wood it consumes" (Jeremiah 5:14). Through their prayer, preaching, and courage in suffering, these witnesses will gall and wound the very hearts and consciences of many of their persecutors, who will go away self-condemned, and even be terrors to themselves. They will be like Pashur at the words of the prophet Jeremiah: "The next day, when Pashur released him from the stocks, Jeremiah said to him, 'The Lord's name for you is not Pashur, but Magor-Missabib. For this is what the Lord says: "I will make you a terror to yourself and to all your friends; with your own eyes you will see them fall by the sword of their enemies"'" (Jeremiah 20:3-4).

These men have power to shut up the sky so that it will not rain during the time they are prophesying; and they have power to turn the waters into blood and to strike the earth with every kind of plague as often as they want (verse 6). In answer to their prayers, God will bring plagues and judgments on their enemies, as he did on Pharaoh, turning their rivers into blood. He will make it not rain for many days and will shut the heavens, restraining the dews of heaven, just as he did in answer to Elijah's prayers. "Now Elijah the Tishbite, from Tishbe in Gilead, said to Ahab, 'As the LORD, the God of Israel, lives, whom I serve, there will be neither dew nor rain in the next few years except at my word'" (1 Kings 17:1). God has ordained his arrows for persecutors and often sends plagues on them while they are persecuting his people. They find it hard to kick against the goads (see Acts 26:9-18).

6. The killing of the witnesses, to make their testimony even stronger. They must seal it with their blood. Notice here:

a. When they will be killed. **Now when they have finished their testimony, the beast that comes up from the Abyss will attack them, and overpower and kill them** (verse 7). **When they have finished their testimony.** They are immortal, they are invulnerable, until their work is completed. Some think these words should be translated, "when they were about to finish their testimony"; that is, when they had prophesied in sackcloth for the greatest part of the 1,260 years, then they would feel the last effect of the antichrist's malice.

b. The enemy that would overcome and kill them. **The beast that comes up from the Abyss will attack them, and overpower and kill them.** Antichrist, the great instrument of the devil, will wage war on them, not only with the arms of subtle philosophy, but mainly with open force and violence. God will permit his enemies to prevail against his witnesses for a time.

c. The barbaric use of the bodies of these killed witnesses. **Their bodies will lie in the street of the great city, which is figuratively called Sodom and Egypt, where also their Lord was crucified** (verse 8). The malice of their enemies was not satisfied with their blood and death but pursued even their dead **bodies.**

First, they would not allow them a quiet burial. Their **bodies** were thrown into the open street, the high street of Babylon or the high road leading to the city. This city **is figuratively called Sodom** on account of its wickedness and **Egypt** on account of its idolatry and oppression. Here Christ in his mystical body has suffered more than in any place in the world.

Second, their dead bodies were insulted by the inhabitants of the earth, and their death brought joy to the people of the anti-Christian world. **For three and a half days men from every people, tribe, language and nation will gaze on their bodies and refuse them burial. The inhabitants of the earth will gloat over them and will celebrate by sending each other gifts, because these two prophets had tormented those who live on the earth** (verses 9-10). They were glad to be rid of these witnesses who by their doctrine and example had touched and tormented the consciences of their enemies. These spiritual weapons cut wicked people to the heart and fill them with the greatest rage and malice against the faithful.

7. The resurrection of these witnesses, and the consequences of it. Notice:

a. When they will rise again. **But after the three and a half days a breath of life from God entered them, and they stood on their feet, and terror struck those who saw them** (verse 11). **Three and a half days** is a comparatively short time. This may be a reference to Christ's resurrection, who is the resurrection and the life. "I am the resurrection and the life. He who believes in me will live, even though he dies" (John 11:25). Or this may refer to Lazarus' resurrection on the fourth day, when everyone thought it was impossible. God's witnesses may be slain, but they will rise again—not only in themselves until the general resurrection, but in their successors. God will revive his work when it seems to be dead in the world.

b. The power through which they were raised. **A breath of life from God entered them, and they stood on their feet.** God put courage as well as life into them. God can make dry bones live. It is the Spirit of God who brings life to dead souls and will bring life to the dead bodies of his people.

c. The effect of this on God's enemies. **Terror struck those who saw them.** The reviving of God's work and witnesses will strike terror into the souls of his enemies. Where there is guilt, there is fear; and a persecuting spirit, though cruel, is not a courageous spirit, but a cowardly one. Herod feared John the Baptist.

8. The ascension of the witnesses into heaven, and the consequences of this. **Then they heard a loud voice from heaven saying to them, "Come up here." And they went up to heaven in a cloud, while their enemies looked on. At that very hour there was a severe earthquake and a tenth of the city collapsed. Seven thousand people were killed in the earth-**

quake, and the survivors were terrified and gave glory to the God of heaven (verses 12-13). Notice:

a. The ascension. By **heaven** we may understand either some more eminent station in the church, the kingdom of grace in this world, or a high place in the kingdom of glory above. The former seems to be the meaning. **They went up to heaven in a cloud, while their enemies looked on** (verse 12) is figurative, not literal. It will be a large part of the punishment of persecutors, both in this world and on the great day, that they will see the faithful witnesses of God greatly honored and advanced. They did not attempt to ascend to this honor until God called them and said, **"Come up here"** (verse 12). The Lord's witnesses must wait for their advancement, both in the church and in heaven, until God calls them. They must not be weary of suffering and service, nor too hastily grasp at the reward. They must wait until their Master calls them, and then they may gladly ascend to him.

b. The consequences of their ascension. Their ascension produces a mighty shock and convulsion in antichrist's empire and the fall of **a tenth of the city** (verse 13). Some people think this refers to the beginning of the reformation from popery, when many princes and states escaped from their subjection to Rome. This great work met with great opposition. All the western world felt a great concussion, and anti-Christian interest received a great blow and lost a great deal of ground and following.

This happened, first, by the sword of war that was then drawn. Many of those who fought under the banner of antichrist were killed by it.

Second, by the sword of the Spirit. The fear of God fell on many. They were convicted of their idolatry, errors, and superstition. Through true repentance, and by embracing the truth, they **gave glory to the God of heaven** (verse 13). Thus when God's work and witnesses revive, the devil's work and witnesses fall before him.

Verses 14-19

The second woe has passed; the third woe is coming soon.

The seventh angel sounded his trumpet, and there were loud voices in heaven, which said:

"The kingdom of the world has become the kingdom of our Lord and of his Christ, and he will reign for ever and ever."

And the twenty-four elders, who were seated on their thrones before God, fell on their faces and worshiped God, saying:

"We give thanks to you, Lord God Almighty, who is and who was, because you have taken your great power and have begun to reign. The nations were angry; and your wrath has come. The time has come for judging the dead, and for rewarding your servants the prophets and your saints and those who reverence your name, both small and great—and for destroying those who destroy the earth."

Then God's temple in heaven was opened, and within his temple was seen the ark of his covenant. And there came flashes of lightning, rumblings, peals of thunder, an earthquake and a great hailstorm.

We have here the sounding of the seventh and last trumpet, which is ushered in by the usual warning and demand for attention. The second woe has passed; the third woe is coming soon. The seventh angel sounded his trumpet, and there were loud voices in heaven, which said: "The kingdom of the world has become the kingdom of our Lord and of his Christ, and he will reign for ever and ever" (verses 14-15). This had been suspended for some time, until the apostle had become acquainted with some intervening occurrences of great importance and worthy of his notice and observation. What he had expected he now heard. The seventh angel sounded. Observe here the effects and consequences of this trumpet.

1. Here were loud and joyful acclamations of the saints and angels in heaven. Notice:

a. The subject of their adorations. And the twenty-four elders, who were seated on their thrones before God, fell on their faces and worshiped God (verse 16). They rose from their seats and fell on their faces and worshiped God. They did this with reverence and humility.

b. The manner of their adorations.

(1) They thankfully recognize the right of our God and Saviour to rule and reign over all the world. "The kingdom of the world has become the kingdom of our Lord and of his Christ, and he will reign for ever and ever" (verse 15). This was always so in title, both by creation and by purchase.

(2) They give Christ thanks because he has asserted his rights, exerted his power, and so turned title into possession.

(3) They rejoice that his reign will never end. He will reign for ever and ever" (verse 15), until all enemies are put under his feet. Nobody will ever take the scepter from his hand.

2. Note the angry resentments of the world at these just appearances and actings of God's power. "The nations were angry; and your wrath has come. The time has come for judging the dead, and for rewarding your servants the prophets and your saints and those who reverence your name, both small and great—and for destroying those who destroy the earth" (verse 18). "The nations were angry." Not only had they been angry, but they continued to be so. Their hearts rose up against God, and they met his wrath with their own anger. It was a time when God was taking just revenge on the enemies of his people, recompensing tribulation to those who had caused the trouble. It was a time when he was beginning to reward his people's faithful services and sufferings. Their enemies could not bear this, and they were angry with God, which only increased their guilt and hastened their destruction.

3. Another consequence was the opening of the temple of God in

heaven. **Then God's temple in heaven was opened, and within his temple was seen the ark of his covenant. And there came flashes of lightning, rumblings, peals of thunder, an earthquake and a great hailstorm** (verse 19). **Then God's temple in heaven was opened.** This may mean there is freer communication between heaven and earth—prayer and praises more freely and frequently ascending, and graces and blessings plentifully descending. But it seems to point to the church of God on earth, a heavenly temple. It is an allusion to the various circumstances of things in the first temple. Under the idolatrous and wicked princes, it was shut up and neglected; but under religious and reforming princes, it was opened and visited. So during the power of antichrist, God's temple seemed to be shut up, but it now was opened again. When it was opened, notice:

a. What was seen: **the ark of his covenant.** This was in the Most Holy place. In this ark the tablets of the law were kept. Before Josiah's time, the law of God had been lost but was then found; so in the reign of antichrist, God's law was set aside and made void by their traditions and decrees. The Scriptures were locked up from the people, and they could not look into the divine oracles. Now they are opened; now they are brought out so everyone can see them. This was an unimaginable and invaluable privilege. And this, like **the ark of his covenant,** was a token of God's presence that had returned to his people, as well as of his favor toward them in Jesus Christ, their Propitiation.

b. What was heard and felt there: **there came flashes of lightning, rumblings, peals of thunder, an earthquake and a great hailstorm.** This great blessing of the Reformation was accompanied by very awful providences; by terrible things in righteousness God answered those prayers that were presented in his holy temple that had now been opened. All the great revolutions of the world are conducted from heaven and are answers to the prayers of the saints.

Revelation
Chapter 12

Introduction

It is generally agreed by the most learned expositors that the narratives we have in this and the two following chapters, from the sounding of the seventh trumpet to the pouring out of the bowls, is not a prediction of the things to come, but rather a recapitulation and representation of things past. Just as God wanted the apostle to foresee the future, so he wanted him to review now the past, that he might more fully appreciate them and see the link between prophecy and that providence that is always fulfilling the Scriptures. In this chapter we have an account of the contest between the church and antichrist—the seed of the woman and the seed of the serpent:

1. As it started in heaven (verses 1-14).
2. As it was carried on in the wilderness (verses 15-17).

Verses 1-11

A great and wondrous sign appeared in heaven: a woman clothed with the sun, with the moon under her feet and a crown of twelve stars on her head. She was pregnant and cried out in pain as she was about to give birth. Then another sign appeared in heaven: an enormous red dragon with seven heads and ten horns and seven crowns on his heads. His tail swept a third of the stars out of the sky and flung them to the earth. The dragon stood in front of the woman who was about to give birth, so that he might devour her child the moment it was born. She gave birth to a son, a male child, who will rule all the nations with an iron scepter. And her child was snatched up to God and to his throne. The woman fled into the desert to a place prepared for her by God, where she might be taken care of for 1,260 days.

And there was war in heaven. Michael and his angels fought against the dragon, and the dragon and his angels fought back. But he was not strong enough, and they lost their place in heaven. The great dragon was hurled down—that ancient serpent called the devil, or Satan, who leads the whole world astray. He was hurled to the earth, and his angels with him.

Then I heard a loud voice in heaven say:

"Now have come the salvation and the power and the kingdom of our God, and the authority of his Christ. For the accuser of our brothers, who accuses them before our God day and night, has been hurled down. They overcame him by the blood of the Lamb and by the word of their testimony; they did not love their lives so much as to shrink from death."

Here we see eminently fulfilled that earlier prophecy when God said to the serpent, "I will put enmity between you and the woman, and between your offspring and hers" (Genesis 3:15). You will observe:

1. The attempts of Satan and his agents to stop the church from growing, by devouring her offspring **the moment it was born** (verse 4). This is graphically described with appropriate images.

a. We see how the church is represented in this vision.

(1) **A great and wondrous sign appeared in heaven: a woman clothed with the sun, with the moon under her feet and a crown of twelve stars on her head** (verse 1). The church is seen here as **a woman**, weaker in this world but the spouse of Christ and the mother of the saints.

(2) As **clothed with the sun**, the imputed righteousness of the Lord Jesus Christ, having put on Christ who is the Sun of righteousness. She, by her relationship to Christ, is invested with honorable rights and privileges and shines in his sunlight.

(3) She has **the moon under her feet**—that is, the world. She stands on it but lives above it. Her heart and hope are not set on earthly things, but on the things that are in heaven, where her Head is.

(4) **On her head** she had **a crown of twelve stars**. This is the doctrine of the Gospel preached by the twelve apostles, which is a crown of glory to all true believers.

(5) **She was pregnant and cried out in pain as she was about to give birth** (verse 2). **She was pregnant** and in pain, **about to give birth** to a holy progeny—Christ. She wanted what was begun in the conviction of sinners to end in their conversion; and when the children were about to be born, she desired the strength to bring them forth, that she might see the travail of her soul.

b. How the grand enemy of the church is represented.

(1) **Then another sign appeared in heaven: an enormous red dragon with seven heads and ten horns and seven crowns on his heads** (verse

3). **Dragon** stands for strength and terror, a **red** dragon for fierceness and cruelty.

(2) **With seven heads**—that is, placed on seven hills, as Rome was. Therefore it is probable that pagan Rome is meant here.

(3) Having **ten horns**—that is, divided into ten provinces, as the Roman Empire was by Augustus Caesar.

(4) Having **seven crowns on his heads,** which is later expounded to be the seven kings: "The seven heads are seven hills on which the woman sits. They are also seven kings" (17:9).

(5) **His tail swept a third of the stars out of the sky and flung them to the earth. The dragon stood in front of the woman who was about to give birth, so that he might devour her child the moment it was born** (verse 4). With his tail he swept **a third of the stars out of the sky and flung them to the earth.** This refers to ministers and professors of the Christian religion being turned out of their places and privileges and making them as weak and useless as he could.

(6) Standing **in front of the woman who was about to give birth, so that he might devour her child the moment it was born.** The dragon is very vigilant to crush the Christian religion at birth and to completely stop its growth and existence in the world.

2. The failure of these attempts against the church. For:

a. **She gave birth to a son, a male child, who will rule all the nations with an iron scepter. And her child was snatched up to God and to his throne** (verse 5). She was safely delivered of **a male child,** by which some understand Christ, others Constantine, and others, with greater propriety, a race of true believers, strong and united, resembling Christ and designed, under him, to "rule them with an iron scepter" (2:27). This means to judge the world through their teaching and lives now, and as assessors with Christ at the great day.

b. The child was taken care of. **Her child was snatched up to God and to his throne.** This means that the child was taken into God's special, powerful, and immediate protection. The Christian religion has been from its infancy the special care of the great God and our Saviour Jesus Christ.

c. **The woman fled into the desert to a place prepared for her by God, where she might be taken care of for 1,260 days** (verse 6). The woman was taken care of as well as the child. **The woman fled into the desert to a place prepared for her by God,** both for her safety and her sustenance. The church was in an obscure state, dispersed. This proved to be her security, through the care of divine providence. So her obscure and private state was for a limited time only and would not continue forever.

3. The attempts of the dragon not only prove unsuccessful against the church, but fatal to his own interests. **And there was war in heaven. Michael and his angels fought against the dragon, and the dragon and**

his angels fought back (verse 7). **There was war in heaven.** We see that **heaven** will support the church in its quarrel. Observe here:

a. The center of this war is **in heaven,** that is, in the church, which is the kingdom of heaven on earth. The church is under the care of heaven and has identical interests.

b. The parties. **Michael and his angels** on one side **against the dragon . . . and his angels** on the other side. Christ, the great Angel of the covenant, and his faithful followers fight against Satan and all his instruments. This latter party would be much superior in numbers and outward strength to the other, but the strength of the church lies in having the Lord Jesus for the Captain of their salvation.

c. The success of the battle. **But he was not strong enough, and they lost their place in heaven** (verse 8). The dragon and his angels fought but did not win. There was a great struggle on both sides, but the victory fell to Christ and his church, and the dragon and his angels were not only conquered but **lost their place in heaven. The great dragon was hurled down—that ancient serpent called the devil, or Satan, who leads the whole world astray. He was hurled to the earth, and his angels with him** (verse 9). Pagan idolatry, which was worshiping devils, was chased out of the empire in the time of Constantine.

d. The triumphant song that was composed and used on this occasion. **Then I heard a loud voice in heaven say: "Now have come the salvation and the power and the kingdom of our God, and the authority of his Christ. For the accuser of our brothers, who accuses them before our God day and night, has been hurled down. They overcame him by the blood of the Lamb and by the word of their testimony; they did not love their lives so much as to shrink from death** (verses 10-11). Observe here:

(1) How the conqueror is adored. **"Now have come the salvation and the power and the kingdom of our God, and the authority of his Christ"** (verse 10). God has now shown himself to be a mighty God. Christ has shown himself to be a strong and mighty Saviour. His own arm has brought salvation, and now his kingdom will be greatly enlarged and established. The salvation and strength of the church are all to be ascribed to the King and Head of the church.

(2) How the conquered enemy is described. First, by his malice. He is **the accuser of our brothers,** and he **accuses them before our God day and night** (verse 10). He appears **before God** as an adversary to the church, continually bringing indictments and accusations against them, whether true or false. Thus he accused Job, and thus he accused Joshua the high priest. "Then he showed me Joshua the high priest standing before the angel of the LORD, and Satan standing at his right side to accuse him" (Zechariah 3:1). Although he hates God's presence, he is still prepared to appear there, in order to accuse God's people. Let us therefore take heed

that we give him no reason to accuse us, and that when we do sin we go before the Lord and accuse and condemn ourselves and commit our cause to Christ as our Advocate. Second, by his disappointment and defeat the dragon and all his accusations are cast out, the indictments quashed, and the accuser turned out of the court with just indignation.

(3) How the victory is won. God's servants overcame Satan. First, **by the blood of the Lamb** (verse 11), as the meritorious cause. By dying, Christ destroyed death's power. "Since the children have flesh and blood, he too shared in their humanity so that by his death he might destroy him who holds the power of death—that is, the devil" (Hebrews 2:14). Second, **by the word of their testimony** (verse 11). This was the great instrument of war, "the sword of the Spirit, which is the word of God" (Ephesians 6:17). The Word of God is proclaimed in the resolute, powerful preaching of the everlasting Gospel. "The weapons we fight with are not the weapons of the world. On the contrary, they have divine power to demolish strongholds" (2 Corinthians 10:4).

They demonstrated **the word of their testimony** through their courage and patience in suffering. **They did not love their lives so much as to shrink from death** (verse 11) when the love of life competed with their loyalty to Christ. They did not **love their lives so much** that they were not prepared to give them up to death but were able to lay them down for Christ's cause. The love they had for their own lives was overcome by stronger affections of another nature; and this courage and zeal helped confound their enemies, convince many of those who watched on, confirm the souls of the faithful, and so contribute greatly to this victory.

Verses 12-17

"Therefore rejoice, you heavens and you who dwell in them! But woe to the earth and the sea, because the devil has gone down to you! He is filled with fury, because he knows that his time is short."
When the dragon saw that he had been hurled to the earth, he pursued the woman who had given birth to the male child. The woman was given the two wings of a great eagle, so that she might fly to the place prepared for her in the desert, where she would be taken care of for a time, times and half a time, out of the serpent's reach. Then from his mouth the serpent spewed water like a river, to overtake the woman and sweep her away with the torrent. But the earth helped the woman by opening its mouth and swallowing the river that the dragon had spewed out of his mouth. Then the dragon was enraged at the woman and went off to make war against the rest of her offspring—those who obey God's commandments and hold to the testimony of Jesus.

We have here an account of this war, so happily finished in heaven, or in the church as it was again renewed and carried on in the wilderness, the place to which the church fled and where she had been for some time secured by the special care of her God and Saviour. Notice:

1. **"Therefore rejoice, you heavens and you who dwell in them! But woe to the earth and the sea, because the devil has gone down to you! He is filled with fury, because he knows that his time is short"** (verse 12). The warning is given concerning the distress and calamity that would fall on the inhabitants of the world in general through the **fury** and rage of **the devil.** Although his malice is chiefly directed against God's servants, he is still an enemy of and hates mankind. As he is defeated in his designs against the church, he is resolved to give all the disturbance he can to the world in general. **"Woe to the earth and the sea."** Satan's rage grows so much greater as he is limited in place and time. When he is confined to the wilderness, he comes with greater **fury because he knows that his time is short.**

2. His second attempt on the church, now in the wilderness. **When the dragon saw that he had been hurled to the earth, he pursued the woman who had given birth to the male child** (verse 13). Notice:

a. The care God has taken of his church. **The woman was given the two wings of a great eagle, so that she might fly to the place prepared for her in the desert, where she would be taken care of for a time, times and half a time, out of the serpent's reach** (verse 14). He carried her on the **wings of a great eagle** to a safe place he had provided for her, where she could continue for a certain time. All this is couched in the prophetic imagery found in Daniel. "He will speak against the Most High and oppress his saints and try to change the set times and the laws. The saints will be handed over to him for a time, times and half a time" (Daniel 7:25).

b. The constant malice of the dragon against the church. The church's obscurity could not completely protect her. **Then from his mouth the serpent spewed water like a river, to overtake the woman and sweep her away with the torrent** (verse 15). The old, subtle serpent, who at first lurked in paradise, now follows the church into the wilderness, and **from his mouth . . . spewed water like a river, to overtake the woman and sweep her away with the torrent.** This may refer to a flood of heresy and error, such as was breathed by Arius, Nestorius, Pelagius, and many others, through which God's church was in danger of being overwhelmed and carried away. God's church is in more danger from heretics than from persecutors, and heresies are as much from the devil as open force and violence.

c. The timely help provided for the church in this dangerous situation. **But the earth helped the woman by opening its mouth and swallowing the river that the dragon had spewed out of his mouth** (verse 16). Some people think this refers to the swarms of Goths and Vandals that invaded the Roman Empire and made way for the Arian rulers who otherwise would have been as furious persecutors as the pagans had been and had exercised great cruelties already. But God opened a breach of war, and the **river** was swallowed up, so the church could enjoy some respite. God often sends the sword to avenge the quarrel of his covenant. When people choose new gods, there is danger of war in the cities.

d. The devil, being thus defeated in his designs on the universal church, now turns his rage against particular people and places. **Then the dragon was enraged at the woman and went off to make war against the rest of her offspring—those who obey God's commandments and hold to the testimony of Jesus** (verse 17). His malice against **the woman** pushes him on to **make war against the rest of her offspring.** Some people think this refers to the Albigenses, who were driven by Diocletian into barren and mountainous places and later were cruelly murdered by popish rage and power for several generations. They were persecuted for no other reason than that they were **those who obey God's commandments and hold to the testimony of Jesus..** Their faithfulness to God and Christ in doctrine, worship, and behavior exposed them to the fury of Satan and his followers. Such faithfulness will expose people in the same way until the end of the world, when the last enemy will be destroyed.

Revelation
Chapter 13

Introduction

We have in this chapter a further description of the church's enemies. These are not different enemies from those previously described, but a new description of them that reveals their evil ways more clearly. They are represented as two beasts. The first comes in verses 1-10, and the second in verses 11-18. By the first some understand pagan Rome, and by the second, papal Rome. Other people understand papal Rome to be represented by both beasts, the first in its secular power, and the second in its ecclesiastical power.

Verses 1-10

And the dragon stood on the shore of the sea.

And I saw a beast coming out of the sea. He had ten horns and seven heads, with ten crowns on his horns, and on each head a blasphemous name. The beast I saw resembled a leopard, but had feet like those of a bear and a mouth like that of a lion. The dragon gave the beast his power and his throne and great authority. One of the heads of the beast seemed to have had a fatal wound, but the fatal wound had been healed. The whole world was astonished and followed the beast. Men worshiped the dragon because he had given authority to the beast, and they also worshiped the beast and asked, "Who is like the beast? Who can make war against him?"

The beast was given a mouth to utter proud words and blasphemies and to exercise his authority for forty-two months. He opened his mouth to blaspheme God, and to slander his name and his dwelling place and those who live in heaven. He was given power to make war against the saints and to conquer them. And he was given authority over every tribe, people, language and nation. All inhabitants of the earth will worship the beast—all whose names have not been written in the book of life belonging to the Lamb that was slain from the creation of the world.

He who has an ear, let him hear.

If anyone is to go into captivity, into captivity he will go.

If anyone is to be killed with the sword, with the sword he will be killed.

This calls for patient endurance and faithfulness on the part of the saints.

We have here an account of the rise and progress of the first beast. Notice:

1. The apostle saw the monster: **And the dragon stood on the shore of the sea. And I saw a beast coming out of the sea. He had ten horns and seven heads, with ten crowns on his horns, and on each head a blasphemous name** (verse 1). John himself perhaps stood **on the shore of the sea,** though it is probable he was still in rapture. He thought he was "on the island of Patmos" (1:9), but whether in the body or out of the body, he could not tell.

2. From where the beast came: **I saw a beast coming out of the sea.** Yet, from its description it was more like a land monster. But the more monstrous everything about it was, the more proper an emblem it would be to set forth the mystery of iniquity and tyranny.

3. The form and shape of this beast: **The beast I saw resembled a leopard, but had feet like those of a bear and a mouth like that of a lion. The dragon gave the beast his power and his throne and great authority** (verse 2). For the most part it **resembled a leopard.** But it **had feet like those of a bear and a mouth like that of a lion.** It had ten horns and seven heads, with ten crowns on his horns, and on each head a blasphemous name** (verse 1). It was a most horrid, hideous monster! Some parts of this vision seem to allude to Daniel's vision of the four beasts that represented four monarchs. "In the first year of Belshazzar king of Babylon, Daniel had a dream, and visions passed through his mind as he was lying on his bed. He wrote down the substance of his dream. Daniel said, 'In my vision at night I looked, and there before me were the four winds of heaven churning up the great sea. Four great beasts, each different from the others, came up out of the sea'" (Daniel 7:1-3). One of those beasts was like a lion, another like a bear, and another like a leopard; this beast was sort of a combination of those three, with the fierceness, strength, and swiftness of them all. **The seven heads** and the **ten horns** seem to refer to its several powers. **The ten crowns** seem to refer to its tributary princes. The **blasphemous name** on **each head** proclaims its direct opposition and enmity to God's glory through the promotion of idolatry.

4. The source and spring of his authority: **The dragon gave the beast**

his power and his throne and great authority. He was set up by the devil and was supported by him to do his work and promote his interest. And he gave him all the assistance he could.

5. **One of the heads of the beast seemed to have had a fatal wound, but the fatal wound had been healed. The whole world was astonished and followed the beast** (verse 3). He received **a fatal wound** but was unexpectedly **healed.** Some think this **fatal wound** refers to the abolishing of pagan idolatry. Then the healing of the wound means the introduction of popish idolatry, similar in substance to the former idolatry, but in a new dress that as effectually answers the devil's purpose as the first one did.

6. **Men worshiped the dragon because he had given authority to the beast, and they also worshiped the beast and asked, "Who is like the beast? Who can make war against him?"** (verse 4). Honor and worship were paid to this infernal monster. **The whole world was astonished and followed the beast.** They all admired his power and his actions. **Men worshiped the dragon because he had given authority to the beast, and they also worshiped the beast** (verse 4). They paid honor and subjection to the devil and his instruments and thought no power could withstand his pawns. Such was the great darkness, degeneracy, and madness of the world.

7. How he exercised his infernal power and policy: **The beast was given a mouth to utter proud words and blasphemies and to exercise his authority for forty-two months. He opened his mouth to blaspheme God, and to slander his name and his dwelling place and those who live in heaven. He was given power to make war against the saints and to conquer them. And he was given authority over every tribe, people, language and nation. All inhabitants of the earth will worship the beast—all whose names have not been written in the book of life belonging to the Lamb that was slain from the creation of the world** (verses 5-8). He gained a sort of universal empire in the world. His malice was principally leveled at God—**he opened his mouth to blaspheme God** and those who attend him in heaven (verse 6). He attacked God by making images of him who is invisible and by worshiping them.

Some say **his [God's] dwelling place** (verse 6) refers to the human nature of the Lord Jesus Christ, in which God dwells as in a tabernacle. This is dishonored by the Roman Catholic doctrine of transubstantiation, which will not allow his body to be a true body and puts it into the power of every priest to prepare a body for Christ.

This attack by the beast is also against **those who live in heaven** (verse 6), the glorified saints, by putting them into the place of pagan demons and praying to them. In this way the malice of the devil shows itself against heaven and the blessed inhabitants of heaven. These people are beyond the reach of his power, so all he can do is blaspheme them. But the saints on earth are more exposed to his cruelty, and he is sometimes allowed to triumph over them and trample on them.

8. The limitation of the devil's power and success, both as to time and persons.

a. He is limited in point of time. His reign will continue only for **forty-two months** (verse 5), in the same way as other prophetic characters in the reign of antichrist.

b. He is limited in connection with the people whom he will entirely subject to his will and power—only **all whose names have not been written in the book of life belonging to the Lamb** (verse 8). Christ has chosen a remnant, redeemed by his blood, recorded in his book, and sealed by his Spirit. The devil and antichrist may overcome them physically and take away their natural life, but he is not able to conquer their souls or force them to forsake their Saviour and join his enemies.

9. **He who has an ear, let him hear** (verse 9). Here is a command to take notice of what is said here about the great sufferings and troubles of the church, and the assurance given that when God has accomplished his work on Mount Zion, his refining work, then he will turn his hand against the enemies of his people. **If anyone is to go into captivity, into captivity he will go. If anyone is to be killed with the sword, with the sword he will be killed. This calls for patient endurance and faithfulness on the part of the saints** (verse 10). Those who have killed with the sword will themselves fall by the sword, and those who have led God's people into captivity will themselves be made captive. This is a call for the saints to be people of **patient endurance and faithfulness.** They need patience to endure such great suffering, and faith in the prospect of such a glorious deliverance.

Verses 11-18

Then I saw another beast, coming out of the earth. He had two horns like a lamb, but he spoke like a dragon. He exercised all the authority of the first beast on his behalf, and made the earth and its inhabitants worship the first beast, whose fatal wound had been healed. And he performed great and miraculous signs, even causing fire to come down from heaven to earth in full view of men. Because of the signs he was given power to do on behalf of the first beast, he deceived the inhabitants of the earth. He ordered them to set up an image in honor of the beast who was wounded by the sword and yet lived. He was given power to give breath to the image of the first beast, so that it could speak and cause all who refused to worship the image to be killed. He also forced everyone, small and great, rich and poor, free and slave, to receive a mark on his right hand or on his forehead, so that no one could buy or sell unless he had the mark, which is the name of the beast or the number of his name.

This calls for wisdom. If anyone has insight, let him calculate the number of the beast, for it is man's number. His number is 666.

Those who think the first beast signifies pagan Rome understand this second beast to be papal Rome, which promotes idolatry and tyranny, but in a more soft and lamb-like way. Those who take the first beast to refer to the secular power of the papacy take the second beast to refer to its spiritual and ecclesiastical powers, which act under the guise of religion and piety toward the souls of men. Notice here:

1. The form and shape of this second beast: **Then I saw another beast, coming out of the earth. He had two horns like a lamb, but he spoke like a dragon** (verse 11). Everyone agrees that this must be some great impostor who under the pretense of religion will deceive people's souls. The Roman Catholics think it is Apollonius Tyanaeus, but Dr. More has rejected that opinion and thinks it is the ecclesiastical powers of the papacy. The pope shows **horns like a lamb** when he pretends to be the vicar of Christ on earth, and so is to be vested with his power and authority. But his speech betrays him, for he issues false doctrines and cruel decrees that show him to belong to the **dragon** and not to the Lamb.

2. The power he exercises: **He exercised all the authority of the first beast on his behalf, and made the earth and its inhabitants worship the first beast, whose fatal wound had been healed** (verse 12). **All the authority of the first beast.** He promotes the same interest and pursues the same design in substance (that is, to draw people away from worshiping the true God to worship those who by nature are not gods, and to subject people's souls and consciences to human will and authority, in opposition to God's will). This aim is promoted by popery as well as by paganism, and by the crafty arts of popery as well as by the secular arm, both serving the interests of the devil, though in a different way.

3. The methods employed by the second beast to carry out his purposes. He uses three kinds:

a. **And he performed great and miraculous signs, even causing fire to come down from heaven to earth in full view of men** (verse 13). Through false **miraculous signs** he **deceived the inhabitants of the earth** (verse 14), who worshiped the former beast in this new image or shape that was now made for him. They would pretend to cause **fire to come down from heaven,** just as Elijah did. God sometimes allows his enemies, as he did with the magicians of Egypt, to do things that seem very wonderful, and by which unwary people may be deluded. It is well known that the papal kingdom has supported fake miracles for a long time.

b. Excommunications, anathemas, severe censures. Through these they pretend to cut people off from Christ and cast them into the power of the devil, but in fact they deliver them over to the secular power, so they may be killed. Notwithstanding their vile hypocrisy, they are justly charged with killing those whom they cannot corrupt.

c. By disfranchisement. **Because of the signs he was given power to do on behalf of the first beast, he deceived the inhabitants of the earth. He** ordered them to set up an image in honor of the beast who was wounded by the sword and yet lived. He was given power to give breath to the image of the first beast, so that it could speak and cause all who refused to worship the image to be killed. He also forced everyone, small and great, rich and poor, free and slave, to receive a mark on his right hand or on his forehead, so that no one could buy or sell unless he had the mark, which is the name of the beast or the number of his name (verses 14-17). They do not allow anyone to enjoy natural, civil rights unless they worship the beast, that is, the image of the pagan beast. To qualify for buying and selling the rights of nature, as well as for positions of profit and trust, they must have the mark of the beast on their forehead or on their right hand (see verse 16); they must have the name of the beast and the number of the beast (see verses 17-18).

It is probable that the mark, the name, and the number of the beast all mean the same thing—that they make up an open profession of subjection and obedience to the papacy, which is receiving the mark on their forehead, and that they oblige themselves to use all their interest, power, and endeavor to promote papal authority, which is receiving the mark on their right hand. We are told that Pope Martin V, in his bull added to the Council of Constance, forbids Roman Catholics to allow any heretics to live in their countries or to make any bargains, follow any trades, or hold any civil offices. This is a very clear interpretation of this prophecy.

4. **This calls for wisdom. If anyone has insight, let him calculate the number of the beast, for it is man's number. His number is 666** (verse 18). We have here **the number of the beast** given in such a way as to show the infinite wisdom of God and to sufficiently exercise the wisdom and accuracy of men. **It is man's number**, computed in the usual way that men calculate, and it **is 666**. Whether this is the number of the errors and heresies that are contained in popery or rather, as others believe, the number of the years from its rise to its fall, it is not certain. It is even less clear what that period is that is described by these prophetic numbers. The most admired dissertation on this intricate subject is by Dr. Potter. It seems to me to be one of those seasons that God has reserved for his own knowledge only. But this we know: God has written "MENE, MENE, TEKEL, PARSIN" (Daniel 5:25) on all his enemies. He has numbered their days, and they will be finished, but his own kingdom will endure forever.

Revelation
Chapter 14

Introduction

After an account of the great trials and sufferings that God's servants endured, we have now a more pleasant scene opening up. The day is now beginning to dawn, and we have the following depicted here:

1. The Lord Jesus at the head of his faithful followers (verses 1-6).
2. Three angels sent successively to proclaim the fall of Babylon and the things prior to and following so great an event (verses 7-13).
3. The vision of the harvest (verses 14-20).

Verses 1-5

Then I looked, and there before me was the Lamb, standing on Mount Zion, and with him 144,000 who had his name and his Father's name written on their foreheads. And I heard a sound from heaven like the roar of rushing waters and like a loud peal of thunder. The sound I heard was like that of harpists playing their harps. And they sang a new song before the throne and before the four living creatures and the elders. No one could learn the song except the 144,000 who had been redeemed from the earth. These are those who did not defile themselves with women, for they kept themselves pure. They follow the Lamb wherever he goes. They were purchased from among men and offered as firstfruits to God and the Lamb. No lie was found in their mouths; they are blameless.

Here we have one of the most pleasing sights that can be viewed in the world—the Lord Jesus Christ at the head of his faithful followers. Notice:

1. How Christ appears: **Then I looked, and there before me was the Lamb, standing on Mount Zion, and with him 144,000 who had his name and his Father's name written on their foreheads** (verse 1).

Mount Zion is the gospel-church. Christ is with his church in the middle of all her troubles, and therefore she is not consumed. It is his presence that secures her perseverance. He appears as a **Lamb**, the true Lamb, the paschal Lamb, to show that his mediatorial government is the fruit of his sufferings and reason for his people's safety and security.

2. How he appears: very honorably.

a. As for the number of people, there are very many—all who are sealed. Not one of them is lost in all the tribulations through which they have gone.

b. Their distinguishing badge: they **had his name and his Father's name written on their foreheads.** They had made a bold and open profession of their faith in God and in Christ. This is followed by appropriate actions, and they are known and approved.

c. **And they sang a new song before the throne and before the four living creatures and the elders. No one could learn the song except the 144,000 who had been redeemed from the earth** (verse 3). Their congratulations and songs of praise were peculiar to the **redeemed**. Earlier we read, **I heard a sound from heaven like the roar of rushing waters and like a loud peal of thunder. The sound I heard was like that of harpists playing their harps** (verse 2). Their praises were as loud as **the roar of rushing waters and like a loud peal of thunder.** They were as melodious as **harpists playing their harps.** They were heavenly—**before the throne** (verse 3). The song was **new** (verse 3), suited to the new covenant and to that new and gracious dispensation of providence under which they now were. Their song was a secret kept from other people, and strangers did not interfere with their joy. "Each heart knows its own bitterness, and no one else can share its joy" (Proverbs 14:10). Other people might repeat the words of the **song** (verse 3), but they were strangers to the true meaning and spirit of it.

d. Their character and description:

(1) They are described by their purity and chastity: **These are those who did not defile themselves with women, for they kept themselves pure. They follow the Lamb wherever he goes. They were purchased from among men and offered as firstfruits to God and the Lamb** (verse 4). **These are those who did not defile themselves with women.** They had not defiled themselves either with physical or spiritual adultery. They had kept themselves clean from the abominations of the anti-Christian generation.

(2) By their loyal steadfast adherence to Christ: **They follow the Lamb wherever he goes.** They follow the conduct of his Word, Spirit, and providence, leaving it to him to lead them into whatever duties and difficulties he pleases.

(3) By their former designation to this honor: **They were purchased from among men and offered as firstfruits to God and the Lamb.** Here

is clear evidence of a special redemption. **They were purchased from among men.** Some of the children of men are, by redeeming mercy, distinguished from others. They were **firstfruits to God and the Lamb,** God's choice ones, eminent in every grace, and the earnest of many more who would be followers of them as they were followers of Christ.

(4) By their universal integrity and conscientiousness: **No lie was found in their mouths; they are blameless** (verse 5). Their hearts were right with God. As for their human infirmities, they were freely pardoned in Christ. This is the happy remnant who wait on the Lord Jesus as their Head and Lord. He is glorified in them, and they in him.

Verses 6-12

Then I saw another angel flying in midair, and he had the eternal gospel to proclaim to those who live on the earth—to every nation, tribe, language and people. He said in a loud voice, "Fear God and give him glory, because the hour of his judgment has come. Worship him who made the heavens, the earth, the sea and the springs of water."

A second angel followed and said, "Fallen! Fallen is Babylon the Great, which made all the nations drink the maddening wine of her adulteries."

A third angel followed them and said in a loud voice: "If anyone worships the beast and his image and receives his mark on the forehead or on the hand, he, too, will drink of the wine of God's fury, which has been poured full strength into the cup of his wrath. He will be tormented with burning sulfur in the presence of the holy angels and of the Lamb. And the smoke of their torment rises for ever and ever. There is no rest day or night for those who worship the beast and his image, or for anyone who receives the mark of his name." This calls for patient endurance on the part of the saints who obey God's commandments and remain faithful to Jesus.

In this part of the chapter we have three angels or messengers sent from heaven to give notice of the fall of Babylon and of those things that come before and follow that great event.

1. **Then I saw another angel flying in midair, and he had the eternal gospel to proclaim to those who live on the earth—to every nation, tribe, language and people** (verse 6). The first **angel** was sent on an errand before this event, and **he had the eternal gospel to proclaim.** Notice:

a. The Gospel is **the eternal gospel.** It is eternal in its nature and in its consequences. "The grass withers and the flowers fall, because the breath of the LORD blows on them. Surely the people are grass. The grass withers and the flowers fall, but the word of our God stands forever" (Isaiah 40:7-8).

b. To preach **the eternal gospel** is a work fit for an **angel.** Such is the dignity and the difficulty of that work! And yet we have this treasure in earthenware pots.

c. **The eternal gospel** is of great concern to all the world; and as it is the concern of all, it is very much to be desired that it should be made known to all, even **to every nation, tribe, language and people.**

d. **He said in a loud voice, "Fear God and give him glory, because the hour of his judgment has come. Worship him who made the heavens, the earth, the sea and the springs of water"** (verse 7). The Gospel is the great means by which people are brought to **"Fear God and give him glory."** Natural religion is not sufficient to keep up the fear of God, nor to secure for him the glory of men. It is the Gospel that revives the fear of God and retrieves his glory in the world.

e. When idolatry creeps into the churches of God, it is the preaching of the Gospel, along with the power of the Holy Spirit, that turns people away from idols to serve the living God, who is the Creator of **the heavens, the earth, the sea and the springs of water.** To worship any other God besides him who created the world is idolatry.

2. **A second angel followed and said, "Fallen! Fallen is Babylon the Great, which made all the nations drink the maddening wine of her adulteries"** (verse 8). A **second angel** follows the other one and proclaims the actual fall of **Babylon.** The preaching of the everlasting Gospel had shaken the foundations of the anti-Christian world and hastened its downfall. By **Babylon** is generally understood Rome, which was previously called "Sodom and Egypt" (11:8) on account of its wickedness and cruelty. It is now, for the first time in Revelation, called **Babylon,** on account of her pride and idolatry. Notice:

a. What God has foreordained and foretold will happen; this is as certain as if it had already taken place.

b. The greatness of the papal Babylon will not be able to prevent her fall but will make it more dreadful and remarkable.

c. The wickedness of **Babylon** in corrupting, debauching, and intoxicating the nations around her will make her fall just and will declare the righteousness of God in her utter ruin. **"Fallen! Fallen is Babylon the Great, which made all the nations drink the maddening wine of her adulteries."** Her crimes are recited as the just cause for her destruction.

3. **A third angel followed them and said in a loud voice: "If anyone worships the beast and his image and receives his mark on the forehead or on the hand . . .** (verse 9). A **third angel** follows the other two and warns everyone about the divine vengeance that awaits all who obstinately adhere to anti-Christian interest after God has thus proclaimed Babylon's downfall. **He, too, will drink of the wine of God's fury, which has been poured full strength into the cup of his wrath. He will be tormented with burning sulfur in the presence of the holy angels and of the Lamb. And the smoke of their torment rises for ever and ever. There is no rest**

day or night for those who worship the beast and his image, or for any-one who receives the mark of his name" (verses 10-11). If after this threatening against Babylon, in part already executed, any should persist in idolatry, professing subjection to the beast and promoting his cause, they must expect to **drink of the wine of God's fury.** They will be forever miserable in body and soul. Jesus Christ will inflict this punishment on them, and the holy angels will behold it and approve of it.

Idolatry, both pagan and papist, is a damning sin in its own nature and will prove fatal to those who persist in it after fair warning is given by the word of providence. Those who refuse to come out of **Babylon** when called to do so, and who resolve to take part in her sins, must receive her plagues. **This calls for patient endurance on the part of the saints who obey God's commandments and remain faithful to Jesus** (verse 12). The guilt and the ruin of such incorrigible idolaters will serve to set forth the excellency of the patience of the saints. These graces will be rewarded with salvation and glory. When the treachery and rebellion of others will be punished with everlasting destruction, then it will be said, to the honor of the faithful, **this calls for patient endurance.** "You have previously seen their patience exercised; now you see it rewarded."

Verses 13-20

Then I heard a voice from heaven say, "Write: Blessed are the dead who die in the Lord from now on."

"Yes," says the Spirit, "they will rest from their labor, for their deeds will follow them."

I looked, and there before me was a white cloud, and seated on the cloud was one "like a son of man" with a crown of gold on his head and a sharp sickle in his hand. Then another angel came out of the temple and called in a loud voice to him who was sitting on the cloud, "Take your sickle and reap, because the time to reap has come, for the harvest of the earth is ripe." So he who was seated on the cloud swung his sickle over the earth, and the earth was harvested.

Another angel came out of the temple in heaven, and he too had a sharp sickle. Still another angel, who had charge of the fire, came from the altar and called in a loud voice to him who had the sharp sickle, "Take your sharp sickle and gather the clusters of grapes from the earth's vine, because its grapes are ripe." The angel swung his sickle on the earth, gathered its grapes and threw them into the great winepress of God's wrath. They were trampled in the winepress outside the city, and blood flowed out of the press, rising as high as the horses' bridles for a distance of 1,600 stadia.

Here we have the vision of the harvest and vintage, introduced with a solemn preface. Notice:

1. The preface: **Then I heard a voice from heaven say, "Write: Blessed are the dead who die in the Lord from now on." "Yes," says the Spirit, "they will rest from their labor, for their deeds will follow them"** (verse 13). Note here:

a. From where this prophecy about the harvest came. It came **from heaven**, and not from men, and therefore it is definitely true and has great authority.

b. How it was to be preserved and made known: by writing. It was to be a matter of record so that God's people might have recourse to it for their support and comfort at all times.

c. What is principally intended, which is, to show the blessedness of all the faithful saints and servants of God, both in death and after death. **"Blessed are the dead who die in the Lord from now on."** Observe here:

(1) The description of those who are and shall be **blessed.** These people are those who **die in the Lord.** This either means they die in the cause of Christ or die in a state of vital union with Christ; such persons are found in Christ when death comes.

(2) The demonstration of this blessedness: **they will rest from their labor, for their deeds will follow them.**

First, they are **blessed** in their **rest.** They rest from all sin, temptation, sorrow, and persecution. Then the wicked stop being any trouble, and the weary are at rest.

Second, they are **blessed** in their recompense, **for their deeds will follow them.** These deeds do not precede them as their title or purchase, but **follow them** as evidence of their having lived and died **in the Lord.** The memory of them will be pleasant, and the reward glorious, far beyond the merit of all their services and sufferings.

Third, they are happy in the time of their dying, for they have lived to see God's cause reviving, the peace of the church returning, and God's wrath falling on their idolatrous, cruel enemies. Such times are good times to die. They have Simeon's desire: "Sovereign Lord, as you have promised, you now dismiss your servant in peace. For my eyes have seen your salvation" (Luke 2:29-30). All this is ratified and confirmed by the testimony of the Spirit witnessing with their spirits, and by the written Word.

2. We have the vision itself, represented by a harvest and a vintage.

a. By a harvest. **I looked, and there before me was a white cloud, and seated on the cloud was one "like a son of man" with a crown of gold on his head and a sharp sickle in his hand. Then another angel came out of the temple and called in a loud voice to him who was sitting on the cloud, "Take your sickle and reap, because the time to reap has come, for the harvest of the earth is ripe"** (verses 14-15). The harvest is an emblem that sometimes signifies the cutting down of the wicked, when ripe for ruin, by the judgments of God, and sometimes the gathering in of the righteous, when ripe for heaven, by the mercy of God. The harvest in these verses seems to represent God's judgments against the wicked. Notice:

(1) The Lord of the harvest—one so **like a son of man** (verse 14) it must be the Lord Jesus who is described:

First, by the chariot on which he sat: **a white cloud** (verse 14). A cloud that had the bright side turned to the church, no matter how dark it was to the wicked.

Second, he who was seated on the cloud swung his sickle over the earth, and the earth was harvested.

Third, by the instrument of his providence: **a sharp sickle in his hand** (verse 14).

Fourth, by the solicitations he had from **the temple** (verse 15) to carry out this great work. What he did, his people wanted him to do. When he was resolved to do it, he did it in answer to their prayers.

(2) Observe the harvest work. It is to **"Take up your sickle and reap the field"** (verse 15). The sickle is the sword of God's justice; the field is the world; reaping is cutting the inhabitants of the earth down and carrying them off.

b. **The time to reap** (verse 15). That was when the corn was **ripe** (verse 15), when the measure of people's sin is filled up and they are ripe for destruction. The most inveterate enemies of Christ and his church are not destroyed until through their sin they are ripe for ruin, and then he will spare them no longer. He will take his sickle, and the earth will be reaped.

c. A vintage. **Another angel came out of the temple in heaven, and he too had a sharp sickle** (verse 17). Some people think these two harvests are merely two emblems of the same judgment. Other people think they refer to distinct events of providence before the end of all things. Notice:

(1) To whom this vintage work was committed: to **another angel** who **came out of the temple in heaven.** He came from the holiest place of all in heaven.

(2) At whose request this vintage work was undertaken. It was, as before, at the cry of an angel from the temple, the ministers and churches of God on earth.

(3) **Still another angel, who had charge of the fire, came from the altar and called in a loud voice to him who had the sharp sickle, "Take your sharp sickle and gather the clusters of grapes from the earth's vine, because its grapes are ripe"** (verse 18). The work of the vintage is made up of two parts. First, the cutting off, to **gather the clusters of grapes from the earth's vine** that are now **ripe** and ready. **The angel swung his sickle on the earth, gathered its grapes** (verse 19). Second, the angel **threw them into the great winepress.** We are told here, in the first place, what this **winepress** is. This was **the great winepress of God's wrath,** the fire of his indignation, some terrible calamity, probably by sword, shedding the blood of the wicked.

In the second place, we are told where this winepress is. **They were trampled in the winepress outside the city, and blood flowed out of the press, rising as high as the horses' bridles for a distance of 1,600 stadia** (verse 20). The winepress is **outside the city**, where the army lay that came against Babylon. In the third place, we are told the amount of the wine, that is, of the blood that was shed through this judgment. It was in depth **as high as the horses' bridles,** and in breadth and length, **1,600 stadia.** Some people say this is 200 Italian miles, which is thought to be the length of the Holy Land and may be meant of the patrimony of the holy see surrounding the city of Rome. But here we are left to doubtful conjectures. Perhaps this great event has not yet been fulfilled, but the vision is for an appointed time. Therefore, though it may seem to delay, we are to wait for it. But who will live when the Lord does this?

Revelation
Chapter 15

Introduction

Until now, according to the judgment of very eminent expositors, God had represented to his servant John:

1. The state of the church under the pagan powers, in the six seals, now opened. Then:
2. The state of the church under the papal powers, in the vision of the six trumpets that began to sound as the seventh seal was opened. Then is inserted:
3. A more general and brief account of the past, present, and future state of the church in the little book. He now proceeds:
4. To show John how antichrist is to be destroyed and by what steps that destruction will be accomplished, in the vision of the seven bowls.

Chapter 15 contains an awe-inspiring introduction or preparation to the pouring out of the bowls, in which we have:

1. A sight of those angels in heaven who were to carry out this great work, and with what acclamations of joy the heavenly hosts applauded the great design (verses 1-5).
2. A sight of these angels coming out of heaven to receive the bowls they were to pour out, and the great commotion that this caused in the world (verses 6-8).

Verses 1-4

I saw in heaven another great and marvelous sign: seven angels with the seven last plagues—last, because with them God's wrath is com-

pleted. **And I saw what looked like a sea of glass mixed with fire and, standing beside the sea, those who had been victorious over the beast and his image and over the number of his name.** They held harps given them by God and sang the song of Moses the servant of God and the song of the Lamb:

"Great and marvelous are your deeds, Lord God Almighty. Just and true are your ways, King of the ages. Who will not fear you, O Lord, and bring glory to your name? For you alone are holy. All nations will come and worship before you, for your righteous acts have been revealed."

Here we have the preparation for the pouring out of the seven bowls, which was committed to seven angels. **I saw in heaven another great and marvelous sign: seven angels with the seven last plagues—last, because with them God's wrath is completed** (verse 1). Exactly how these **angels** appeared to the apostle **in heaven** we do not know. But we know it was in a wonderful manner, for several reasons:

1. Because of the work they had to do: to finish the destruction of the antichrist. God was now about to pour out his **seven last plagues.** As the measure of Babylon's sins was filled up, its people would now experience the full measure of his vindictive wrath.

2. **And I saw what looked like a sea of glass mixed with fire and, standing beside the sea, those who had been victorious over the beast and his image and over the number of his name. They held harps given them by God** (verse 2). The spectators and witnesses of their commission were **those who had been victorious over the beast and his name.** These people stood on **a sea of glass,** representing, as some think, this world, a brittle thing that will be broken into pieces. Others think this is the Gospel covenant, alluding to the bronze bowl, or sea, in the temple, in which the priests were to wash. God's faithful servants stand on the foundation of Christ's righteousness. Other people think this is the Red Sea that stood, as it were, congealed while the Israelites went through. The pillar of fire reflected light on the waters so that it **looked like a sea of glass mixed with fire.** This is to show the fire of God's wrath against Pharaoh and so his horses would dissolve in the congealed waters and be destroyed in this way. **And sang the song of Moses the servant of God and the song of the Lamb: "Great and marvelous are your deeds, Lord God Almighty. Just and true are your ways, King of the ages"** (verse 3). There seems to be an allusion to this in the song the Israelites sang after walking through the sea. They **sang the song of Moses,** in which:

a. They extolled the greatness of God's works and the justice and truth of his ways, both in delivering his people and in destroying their enemies. They rejoiced in hope and in the close prospect they had of this, though their deliverance had not yet happened.

b. They called on all nations to give to God the fear, glory, and worship that were due to such a discovery of his truth and justice. **Who will not fear you, O Lord, and bring glory to your name? For you alone are holy. All nations will come and worship before you, for your righteous acts have been revealed"** (verse 4).

Verses 5-8

After this I looked and in heaven the temple, that is, the tabernacle of Testimony, was opened. Out of the temple came the seven angels with the seven plagues. They were dressed in clean, shining linen and wore golden sashes around their chests. Then one of the four living creatures gave to the seven angels seven golden bowls filled with the wrath of God, who lives for ever and ever. And the temple was filled with smoke from the glory of God and from his power, and no one could enter the temple until the seven plagues of the seven angels were completed.

Notice:

1. How these angels appeared. They came out of heaven to carry out their commission. **After this I looked and in heaven the temple, that is, the tabernacle of Testimony, was opened** (verse 5). Here is an allusion to the holiest of all in the **tabernacle** and **temple**, where resided the mercy-seat, covering the ark of the testimony, and also where the high priest made intercession, and God communed with his people and heard their prayers. By this, as it is here mentioned, we may understand:

a. In God's judgments that were now about to take place on the antichrist and company, he was fulfilling the promises and prophecies of his Word and covenant, which were always before him and of which he was always mindful.

b. In this work he was answering the prayers of the people that were offered to him by their great High Priest.

c. God was in this avenging the quarrel of his own Son, our Saviour Jesus Christ, whose offices and authority had been usurped, his name dishonored, and the great purposes of his death opposed by antichrist and his adherents.

d. He was opening a wider door of freedom for his people to worship him in numerous solemn assemblies, without the fear of their enemies.

2. How they were equipped and prepared for their work. Notice:

a. Their array: **Out of the temple came the seven angels with the seven plagues. They were dressed in clean, shining linen and wore golden sashes around their chests** (verse 6). This was the dress of the high priests when they went in to inquire of God and came out with an answer from him. This showed that these angels were acting in all things under divine appointment and direction, and that they were going to "gather together for the great supper of God" (19:17). The angels are the ministers of divine justice, and they do everything in a pure and holy manner.

b. Their method, what it was, and where they received it from: **Then one of the four living creatures gave to the seven angels seven golden bowls filled with the wrath of God, who lives for ever and ever** (verse 7). The method by which they were to carry out this work was **seven gold bowls filled with the wrath of God** against his enemies. The meanest creature, when armed with God's anger, will be too hard for any army in the world, but even more God's angels. God's wrath was not to be poured out all at once but was divided into seven parts that would successively fall on the anti-Christian party. From where did the angels receive these bowls? From **one of the four living creatures,** one of the ministers of the true church—that is, in answer to the prayers of the ministers and the people of God, to avenge their cause, in which the angels are willingly employed.

c. **And the temple was filled with smoke from the glory of God and from his power, and no one could enter the temple until the seven plagues of the seven angels were completed** (verse 8). Ponder the impression these things made on all who stood near **the temple.** They were all, as it were, covered in clouds of **smoke** that **filled** the temple with the glorious and powerful presence of God. So **no one could enter the temple until** the work was completed. The interests of antichrist were so interwoven with the civil interests of the nations that he could not be destroyed without giving a great shock to the world. God's people would have but little rest and leisure to assemble themselves before him while this great work was carrying on. For the present their sabbaths would be interrupted, ordinances of public worship intermittent, and all thrown into a general confusion. God himself was now preaching to the church, and to all the world, by terrible things in righteousness; but when this work was finished, the churches would have rest, the temple would be opened, and the solemn assemblies gathered, edified, and multiplied. The greatest deliverances of the church are brought about by awful and astonishing steps of providence.

Revelation
Chapter 16

Introduction

In this chapter we have an account of the pouring out of these bowls that were filled with God's wrath. The seven were poured over the whole anti-Christian empire and on everything linked to it:

#1 On the earth (verse 2).
#2 On the sea (verse 3).
#3 On the rivers and springs of water (verse 4). Here the heavenly hosts proclaim and applaud the righteousness of the judgments of God.
#4 Over the sun (verse 8).
#5 On the throne of the beast (verses 10-11).
#6 On the river Euphrates (verse 12).
#7 On the air; thus the cities of the nations fell, and great Babylon came in remembrance before God (verses 17-21).

Verses 1-7

Then I heard a loud voice from the temple saying to the seven angels, "Go, pour out the seven bowls of God's wrath on the earth."

The first angel went and poured out the bowl on the land, and ugly and painful sores broke out on the people who had the mark of the beast and worshiped his image.

The second angel poured out his bowl on the sea, and it turned into blood like that of a dead man, and every living thing in the sea died.

The third angel poured out his bowl on the rivers and springs of water, and they became blood. Then I heard the angel in charge of the waters say:

"You are just in these judgments, you who are and who were, the

Holy One, because you have so judged; for they have shed the blood of your saints and prophets, and you have given them blood to drink as they deserve."

And I heard the altar respond:

"Yes, Lord God Almighty, true and just are your judgments."

In the previous chapter we saw the great and solemn preparation that was made for the pouring out of the bowls. Now this takes place. Notice:

1. Though everything was made ready before, yet nothing was to happen without an immediate positive order from God. And this he gave from the temple, in answer to the prayers of his people, thus avenging their quarrel.

2. No sooner was the word of command given than it was immediately obeyed. No delay or objection was made. We find that some of the best men, such as Moses and Jeremiah, did not so readily comply with God's call. But God's angels excel not only in strength, but in a readiness to do God's will. **Then I heard a loud voice from the temple saying to the seven angels, "Go, pour out the seven bowls of God's wrath on the earth"** (verse 1). God says, **"Go, pour our the seven bowls,"** and at once the work starts. We are taught to pray that the will of God may be done on earth as it is in heaven.

Now we come to a series of very terrible dispensations of providence, about which it is difficult to give the certain meaning or to make the particular application. But in general it is worth noticing the following:

a. We have here a reference and allusion to several of the plagues of Egypt, such as turning the water into blood and the plague of painful sores. Their sins were similar, and so were their punishments.

b. These bowls have an obvious reference to the seven trumpets, which represented the rise of antichrist. From this we learn that the fall of the church's enemies will bear some resemblance to their rise. God can bring them down in the same ways that they chose to exalt themselves. The fall of antichrist will be gradual; as Rome was not built in one day, so neither shall it fall in one day, but by degrees. It will fall so that it can rise no more.

c. The fall of anti-Christian leaders and their followers will be universal. Everything that belongs to them in any way or could be useful to them in any way are liable to destruction. Their earth, their air, their sea, their rivers, their cities are consigned to ruin, all accursed for the sake of their wickedness. Thus the creation groans and suffers because of the sins of men. Now we will notice:

(1) The first angel who poured out his bowl. **The first angel went and poured out the bowl on the land, and ugly and painful sores broke out on the people who had the mark of the beast and worshiped his image** (verse 2). Notice, first, where it fell: **on the land.** That is, some say, on

ordinary people; others say it fell on the Roman clergy, who were the basis of the papacy and of the earthly split, all carrying on earthly purposes.

Second, what it produced: **ugly and painful sores broke out on the people who had the mark of the beast.** They had marked themselves because of their sin, and now God marks them out by his judgments. These sores, some think, signify some of the first appearances of providence against their state and interest, which gave them great uneasiness, for it revealed their inner turmoil and was a token of further evil. The tokens of the plagues had arrived.

(2) **The second angel poured out his bowl on the sea, and it turned into blood like that of a dead man, and every living thing in the sea died** (verse 3). **The second angel poured out his bowl,** and here we see:

First, where it fell: **on the sea.** That is, some say, on the jurisdiction and dominion of the papacy. Others think it refers to the whole system of their religion, their false doctrines, superstitious rites, idolatrous worship, pardons, indulgences, and a great mass of wicked inventions and institutions through which they maintain a trade to their own advantage, but harmful to all who deal with them.

Second, what it produced: **it turned into blood like that of a dead man, and every living thing in the sea died.** God not only uncovered the vanity and falseness of their religion, but its pernicious and deadly nature—namely, that people's souls were poisoned by what pretended to be the certain means of their salvation.

(3) **The third angel poured out his bowl on the rivers and springs of water, and they became blood** (verse 4). We are told, first, where it fell: **on the rivers and springs of water.** That is, some very learned men say, on their emissaries, and especially the Jesuits who, like streams, conveyed the venom and poison of their errors and idolatries from the source right through the earth.

Second, what effect it had on them: **they became blood.** Some think it stirred up Christian princes to take just revenge on those who had been the great incendiaries of the world and had caused the shedding of blood of armies and of martyrs. The following doxology supports this interpretation: **Then I heard the angel in charge of the waters say: "You are just in these judgments, you who are and who were, the Holy One, because you have so judged; for they have shed the blood of your saints and prophets, and you have given them blood to drink as they deserve"** (verses 5-6). The instrument that God makes use of in this work is called **the angel in charge of the waters** (verse 5), who exalts the righteousness of God in this retaliation: **"for they have shed the blood of your saints and prophets, and you have given them blood to drink as they deserve"** (verse 6). Another angel replies in full agreement: **And I heard the altar respond: "Yes, Lord God Almighty, true and just are your judgments"** (verse 7).

Verses 8-11

The fourth angel poured out his bowl on the sun, and the sun was given power to scorch people with fire. They were seared by the intense heat and they cursed the name of God, who had control over these plagues, but they refused to repent and glorify him.

The fifth angel poured out his bowl on the throne of the beast, and his kingdom was plunged into darkness. Men gnawed their tongues in agony and cursed the God of heaven because of their pains and their sores, but they refused to repent of what they had done.

In these verses we see the work continuing in the appointed order.

The fourth angel poured out his bowl on the sun, and the sun was given power to scorch people with fire (verse 8). The fourth angel poured out his bowl, and its contents fell on the sun. Some say the sun denotes some eminent prince of popish commission who would renounce the false religion a little while before its utter downfall. Some say it is the German emperor. And what will be the consequence of this? They were seared by the intense heat and they cursed the name of God, who had control over these plagues, but they refused to repent and glorify him (verse 9). The sun that had previously cherished them with warm and benign influences will now become hot against idolaters and will scorch them. Princes will use their power and authority to suppress them. But this, far from bringing them to repentance, causes them to curse the name of God and their King and look upward as they throw out blasphemous words against the God of heaven. They were hardened to their own ruin.

The fifth angel poured out his bowl on the throne of the beast, and his kingdom was plunged into darkness. Men gnawed their tongues in agony and cursed the God of heaven because of their pains and their sores, but they refused to repent of what they had done (verses 10-11). The fifth angel poured out his bowl (verse 10). Notice:

1. Where it fell: on the throne of the beast (verse 10), upon Rome itself, the mystical Babylon, the head of the anti-Christian empire.

2. What effect it had there: the whole kingdom of the beast was plunged into darkness and distress. The very city that was the center of their policy, the source of all their learning and all their knowledge and all their pomp and pleasure, now becomes a source of darkness, pain, and anguish. Darkness was one of the plagues of Egypt, and it is opposed to luster and honor and so forebodes the contempt and scorn to which the anti-Christian interest would be exposed. Darkness is opposed to wisdom and discernment and forebodes the confusion and folly that the idolaters would then discover. Darkness is opposed to pleasure and joy, and so signifies their anger and vexation of spirit when their calamities thus came upon them.

Verses 12-16

The sixth angel poured out his bowl on the great river Euphrates, and its water was dried up to prepare the way for the kings from the East. Then I saw three evil spirits that looked like frogs; they came out of the mouth of the dragon, out of the mouth of the beast and out of the mouth of the false prophet. They are spirits of demons performing miraculous signs, and they go out to the kings of the whole world, to gather them for the battle on the great day of God Almighty.

"Behold, I come like a thief! Blessed is he who stays awake and keeps his clothes with him, so that he may not go naked and be shamefully exposed."

Then they gathered the kings together to the place that in Hebrew is called Armageddon.

We read here: **The sixth angel poured out his bowl on the great river Euphrates, and its water was dried up to prepare the way for the kings from the East** (verse 12). Notice:

1. Where it fell—**on the great river Euphrates.** Some take this literally to mean the place where the Turkish empire began. They think this is a prophecy about the destruction of the Turkish monarchy and idolatry, which they think will happen at about the same time as the destruction of the papacy, which is another antichrist. In this way a pathway will be cleared for the Jews to come back, whose princes are in the east. Others take it for the river Tiber, for as Rome is mystical Babylon, Tiber is mystical **Euphrates.** And when Rome is destroyed, her river and merchandise must suffer with her.

2. What did this bowl produce?

a. The drying up of the river that furnished the city with wealth, provisions, and all sorts of accommodations.

b. A way is thereby prepared **for the kings from the East.** The idolatry of the church of Rome has been a great hindrance both to the conversion of the Jews, who have been long cured of their inclination to idols, and of Gentiles, who are hardened in their idolatry. It is therefore very probable that the downfall of popery, removing these obstacles, will open a way for both the Jews and other eastern nations to come into Christ's church. And if we think Muslims will fall at the same time, there will be even more open communication between the western and eastern nations, which may facilitate the conversion of the Jews and the fullness of the Gentiles. And when this work of God appears and is about to be accomplished, it will be no surprise if it ushers in another consequence:

c. The last effort of the great dragon. He is resolved to have another attempt so that, if possible, he may retrieve the ruinous posture of his affairs in the world. He is now rallying his forces, recollecting all his spirits, to make one desperate effort before everything is lost. This is occasioned by the pouring out of the sixth seal.

Then I saw three evil spirits that looked like frogs; they came out of the mouth of the dragon, out of the mouth of the beast and out of the mouth of the false prophet (verse 13). Notice here:

First, the instruments he makes use of to engage the powers of the earth in his cause and quarrel: **three evil spirits that looked like frogs.** One comes **out of the mouth of the dragon,** another **out of the mouth of the beast,** and a third **out of the mouth of the false prophet.** Hell, the secular power of the antichrist, and his ecclesiastical power all combine to send their several instruments, furnished with hellish malice, with worldly policy, and with religious falsehood and deceit. These will collect together the devil's forces for a decisive battle.

Second, the means these instruments would use to engage the powers of the earth in this war: **They are spirits of demons performing miraculous signs, and they go out to the kings of the whole world, to gather them for the battle on the great day of God Almighty** (verse 14). They will perform fake **miraculous signs.** This is an old ploy of the devil. "The coming of the lawless one will be in accordance with the work of Satan displayed in all kinds of counterfeit miracles, signs and wonders, and in every sort of evil that deceives those who are perishing" (2 Thessalonians 2:9-10). Some think that a short time before the fall of the antichrist, the popish pretense of power to work miracles will be revived and will very much amuse and deceive the world.

Third, the place of the battle, **Armageddon** (verse 16), is, some say, Mount Megiddo, near which, from a stream coming from it, Barak overcame Sisera and all the kings allied with him (Judges 5:19). In the valley of Megiddo Josiah was killed also. This place has been famous for two events of a very different nature. The first event is very happy for God's church, but the second is very unhappy for it. It will now be the field in which the church will be engaged, and she will be victorious. This battle requires time to be prepared, and therefore further account of it is delayed until 19:19-20.

Fourth, the warning that God gives about this great and decisive trial, to engage his people to prepare for it: **"Behold, I come like a thief! Blessed is he who stays awake and keeps his clothes with him, so that he may not go naked and be shamefully exposed." Then they gathered the kings together to the place that in Hebrew is called Armageddon** (verses 15-16). The battle will be sudden and unexpected, and therefore Christians should be clothed and armed and ready for it, so they are not surprised and ashamed. When God's cause comes to be tried and his battles to be fought, all his people should be prepared to stand up for his interest and to be faithful and valiant in his service.

Verses 17-21

The seventh angel poured out his bowl into the air, and out of the temple came a loud voice from the throne, saying, "It is done!" Then there came flashes of lightning, rumblings, peals of thunder and a severe earthquake. No earthquake like it has ever occurred since man has been on earth, so tremendous was the quake. The great city split into three parts, and the cities of the nations collapsed. God remembered Babylon the Great and gave her the cup filled with the wine of the fury of his wrath. Every island fled away and the mountains could not be found. From the sky huge hailstones of about a hundred pounds each fell upon men. And they cursed God on account of the plague of hail, because the plague was so terrible.

Here we have an account of the seventh and last angel pouring out his bowl, contributing his part toward the accomplishment of the downfall of Babylon, the finishing stroke. Here, as before, notice:

1. **The seventh angel poured out his bowl into the air, and out of the temple came a loud voice from the throne, saying, "It is done!"** (verse 17). Note where the plague fell: **into the air,** on the prince of the power of the air, that is, the devil. His powers were restrained, his activities confounded; he is bound by God's chain; God's sword is on his eye and arm. For the devil, as well as the powers of the earth, is subject to the almighty power of God. He had used all possible means to preserve the anti-Christian interests and to prevent the fall of Babylon. All the influence that he has on people's minds, blinding their judgments and perverting them, hardening their hearts, raising their enmity to the Gospel as much as possible, was exercised. But now here is a bowl poured out on his kingdom, and he is not able to support his tottering cause and interest any longer.

2. What it produced:

a. A thankful voice from heaven, pronouncing that now the work was done. The church triumphant in heaven saw it and rejoiced. The church militant on earth saw it and became triumphant. It is finished.

b. A mighty commotion on the earth. **Then there came flashes of lightning, rumblings, peals of thunder and a severe earthquake. No earthquake like it has ever occurred since man has been on earth, so tremendous was the quake** (verse 18). An **earthquake,** so great that one like it had never **occurred since man has been on earth,** shook the very center of the earth. And this was ushered in through the usual accompanying **flashes of lightning, rumblings, peals of thunder.**

c. The fall of **Babylon** was divided into three parts. **The great city split into three parts, and the cities of the nations collapsed. God remembered Babylon the Great and gave her the cup filled with the wine of the fury of his wrath** (verse 19). Babylon is called **the cities of the nations** because it had ruled over the nations and absorbed the idolatry of the nations, incorporating into her religion something of the Jewish, something of the pagan, and something of the Christian religion, and so was three cities in one. God now remembered this great and wicked city. For some time it appeared that he had forgotten her idolatry and cruelty; yet now he gives her **the cup filled with the wine of the fury of his wrath.** And this downfall extended beyond the center of antichrist. It reached from the center to the circumference. Every island and every mountain, even those that seemed naturally most secure, were carried away in the deluge of this ruin.

3. How the anti-Christian party was affected by this: **Every island fled away and the mountains could not be found. From the sky huge hailstones of about a hundred pounds each fell upon men. And they cursed God on account of the plague of hail, because the plague was so terrible** (verses 20-21). It fell on them as a dreadful storm—**huge hailstones of about a hundred pounds each fell upon men.** It was as if the stones of the city, tossed into the air, fell on their heads, each weighing a hundred pounds. Yet men remained far from repenting and blasphemed God who was punishing them.

Here was a dreadful plague of the heart, a spiritual judgment more dreadful and destructive than all the rest. Notice:

a. The greatest calamities that can befall people will not bring them to repentance, unless God's grace is working in them.

b. Those who do not profit from God's judgments are always worse after them.

c. To be hardened in sin and enmity against God by his righteous judgments is a definite sign of utter destruction.

Revelation
Chapter 17

Introduction

This chapter is another example of those things that had already been revealed concerning the wickedness and ruin of antichrist. This antichrist had been previously depicted as a beast and is now described as a great prostitute. Here:

1. The apostle is invited to see the vile woman (verses 1-2).
2. He tells us what she looked like (verses 3-6).
3. The mystery of it is explained to him (verses 7-12).
4. Her ruin is foretold (verses 13-18).

Verses 1-6

One of the seven angels who had the seven bowls came and said to me, "Come, I will show you the punishment of the great prostitute, who sits on many waters. With her the kings of the earth committed adultery and the inhabitants of the earth were intoxicated with the wine of her adulteries."

Then the angel carried me away in the Spirit into a desert. There I saw a woman sitting on a scarlet beast that was covered with blasphemous names and had seven heads and ten horns. The woman was dressed in purple and scarlet, and was glittering with gold, precious stones and pearls. She held a golden cup in her hand, filled with abominable things and the filth of her adulteries. This title was written on her forehead:
MYSTERY
BABYLON THE GREAT
THE MOTHER OF PROSTITUTES
AND OF THE ABOMINATIONS OF THE EARTH.

I saw that the woman was drunk with the blood of the saints, the blood of those who bore testimony to Jesus.

When I saw her, I was greatly astonished.

Here we have a new vision, not in content, for that is the same as that which came under the last three bowls, but new in its method of description. Notice:

1. The invitation given to the apostle to take a view of what was here to be represented: **One of the seven angels who had the seven bowls came and said to me, "Come, I will show you the punishment of the great prostitute, who sits on many waters"** (verse 1). This is the name of great infamy. A prostitute, in this passage, is someone who is married and has been false to her husband's bed, has forsaken the guide of her youth, and has broken God's covenant. **"With her the kings of the earth committed adultery and the inhabitants of the earth were intoxicated with the wine of her adulteries"** (verse 2). She had been a prostitute with **the kings of the earth**, whom she had **intoxicated with the wine of her adulteries**.

2. The appearance she made: it was bright and gaudy, as such creatures are. **The woman was dressed in purple and scarlet, and was glittering with gold, precious stones and pearls. She held a golden cup in her hand, filled with abominable things and the filth of her adulteries** (verse 4). Here were all the allurements of worldly honor and riches, pomp and pride, suited to sensual and worldly minds.

3. Her principal center and residence: **Then the angel carried me away in the Spirit into a desert. There I saw a woman sitting on a scarlet beast that was covered with blasphemous names and had seven heads and ten horns** (verse 3). **The scarlet beast that was covered with blasphemous names and had seven heads and ten horns** is Rome, the city on seven hills, infamous for idolatry, tyranny, and blasphemy.

4. Her name. **This title was written on her forehead: MYSTERY / BABYLON THE GREAT / THE MOTHER OF PROSTITUTES AND OF THE ABOMINATIONS OF THE EARTH** (verse 5). It was the custom of impudent harlots to hang out signs, with their names, so everyone would know what they were. Notice here:

a. She derives her name from where she lives: **BABYLON THE GREAT.** So we would not mistake it for the old Babylon literally, we are told there is a **MYSTERY** in her name. It is some other city resembling the old Babylon.

b. She is named after her infamous way of life: she is not only a prostitute, but **THE MOTHER OF PROSTITUTES.** She breeds, nurses, and trains others in the ways of idolatry and in all sorts of immoral and wicked practices. She is the parent and nurse of all false religion and filthy conversation.

c. Her diet: **I saw that the woman was drunk with the blood of the saints, the blood of those who bore testimony to Jesus. When I saw her**

I was greatly astonished (verse 6). She sated herself with **the blood of the saints, and the blood of those who bore testimony to Jesus.** She drank their blood with such greediness that she intoxicated herself with it. She enjoyed it so much that she could not tell when she'd had enough of it. She was satiated but never satisfied.

Verses 7-13

Then the angel said to me: "Why are you astonished? I will explain to you the mystery of the woman and of the beast she rides, which has the seven heads and ten horns. The beast, which you saw, once was, now is not, and will come up out of the Abyss and go to his destruction. The inhabitants of the earth whose names have not been written in the book of life from the creation of the world will be astonished when they see the beast, because he once was, now is not, and yet will come.

"This calls for a mind with wisdom. The seven heads are seven hills on which the woman sits. They are also seven kings. Five have fallen, one is, the other has not yet come; but when he does come, he must remain for a little while. The beast who once was, and now is not, is an eighth king. He belongs to the seven and is going to his destruction.

"The ten horns you saw are ten kings who have not yet received a kingdom, but who for one hour will receive authority as kings along with the beast. They have one purpose and will give their power and authority to the beast."

Here we have the mystery of this vision explained. **Then the angel said to me: "Why are you astonished? I will explain to you the mystery of the woman and of the beast she rides, which has the seven heads and ten horns"** (verse 7). The apostle wondered at the sight of this woman. The angel undertakes to open this vision to him, it being the key to the previous visions; and he tells the apostle what was meant by the beast on which the woman sat. But it is explained in such a way that it needs further explanation.

1. **"The beast, which you saw, once was, now is not, and will come up out of the Abyss and go to his destruction. The inhabitants of the earth whose names have not been written in the book of life from the creation of the world will be astonished when they see the beast, because he once was, now is not, and yet will come"** (verse 8). This beast **was, now is not, and will come.** That is, it was a center of idolatry and persecution. **Now is not**—that is, not in the ancient form, which was pagan. **And will come**—that is, it is truly the center of idolatry and tyranny, but of another kind. **Will come up out of the Abyss** (verse 7). Idolatry and cruelty come from hell and will return there.

2. **"This calls for a mind with wisdom. The seven heads are seven hills**

on which the woman sits" (verse 9). The beast had **seven heads**; this phrase has a double meaning.

a. **Seven hills.** These are the seven hills on which Rome stands.

b. "**They are also seven kings. Five have fallen, one is, the other has not yet come; but when he does come, he must remain for a little while**" (verses 9-10). **Seven kings.** These are seven kinds of government. Rome was governed by kings, consuls, tribunes, decemviri, dictators, pagan emperors, and Christian emperors. Five of these no longer lived when this prophecy was written. One was still in being, the pagan emperor; and the other, that is, the Christian emperor, was still to come. **Five have fallen, one is, the other has not yet come.** This beast, the papacy, makes an eighth ruler and sets up idolatry again.

3. The beast had **ten horns** (verse 7). "**The ten horns you saw are ten kings who have not yet received a kingdom, but who for one hour will receive authority as kings along with the beast**" (verse 12). The **ten horns** are said to be the "**ten kings who have not yet received a kingdom.**" **Not yet**; that is, some say, the ten kings will not rise up until toward the end of antichrist's reign, and then they will reign only, as it were, **for one hour . . . with the beast.** But during that time they will be very zealous to be totally devoted to the work and interests of the papacy.

Verses 14-18

"**They will make war against the Lamb, but the Lamb will overcome them because he is Lord of lords and King of kings—and with him will be his called, chosen and faithful followers.**"

Then the angel said to me, "The waters you saw, where the prostitute sits, are peoples, multitudes, nations and languages. The beast and the ten horns you saw will hate the prostitute. They will bring her to ruin and leave her naked; they will eat her flesh and burn her with fire. For God has put it into their hearts to accomplish his purpose by agreeing to give the beast their power to rule, until God's words are fulfilled. The woman you saw is the great city that rules over the kings of the earth."

Here we have an account of the downfall of Babylon, which is described in more detail in the next chapter.

1. Here is a war that has started between the beast and his followers and the Lamb and his followers: "**They will make war against the Lamb, but the Lamb will overcome them because he is Lord of lords and King of kings—and with him will be his called, chosen and faithful followers**" (verse 14). The beast and his army, to the human eye, seem to be much stronger than the Lamb and his army. One would not imagine that an army led by a Lamb could stand against the great red dragon!

2. But here is a victory gained by the Lamb: "**The Lamb will overcome**

them." Christ must rule, and all his enemies will be put under his feet. He will be sure to meet with many enemies and much opposition, but he will also be sure to win the victory.

3. Here is the ground and reason of this certain victory. It is due to:

a. The character of the Lamb. **"He is Lord of lords and King of kings."** He has, both by nature and by office, supreme devotion and power over all things. All the powers of earth and heaven are subject to his check and control.

b. The character of his followers. They are his **called, chosen and faithful followers.** They are called out by commission to the warfare, they are chosen and fitted for it, and they will be faithful in it. Such an army, under such a Commander, will at length carry all the world before them.

4. The victory is justly acknowledged:

a. By the vast multitude who paid obedience and subjection to the beast and to the prostitute. **Then the angel said to me, "The waters you saw, where the prostitute sits, are peoples, multitudes, nations and languages"** (verse 15). **The prostitute sits**—that is, presides over—**the waters.** These **waters** are many multitudes of people and nations, of all languages. She reigned not only over kingdoms, but over the kings, and they were vassals. **"The woman you saw is the great city that rules over the kings of the earth"** (verse 18).

b. By the powerful influence that God showed that he had over the minds of great men. Their hearts were in his hand, and he turned them as he pleased. For:

(1) **"The beast and the ten horns you saw will hate the prostitute. They will bring her to ruin and leave her naked; they will eat her flesh and burn her with fire. For God has put it into their hearts to accomplish his purpose by agreeing to give the beast their power to rule, until God's words are fulfilled"** (verses 16-17). It was of God, and to fulfill his will, that these kings agreed **to give the beast their power to rule** (verse 17). They were judicially blinded and hardened to do so.

(2) After their hearts were turned against the prostitute to hate her, and they brought her to ruin and left her naked, God brought them to see their folly and how they had been bewitched and enslaved by the papacy. It was out of just resentment that they not only deserted Rome but would be made the instruments of God's providence in her destruction.

Revelation
Chapter 18

Introduction

We have here:

1. An angel proclaiming the fall of Babylon (verses 1-2).
2. Assigning the reasons for her fall (verse 3).
3. Giving warning to all who belonged to God to come out of her (verses 4-5) and to assist her judgment (verses 6-8).
4. The great lamentation made for her by those who had shared in her sinful pleasures (verses 9-19).
5. The great joy there would be among others at the sight of her irrecoverable ruin (verses 20-24).

Verses 1-3

After this I saw another angel coming down from heaven. He had great authority, and the earth was illuminated by his splendor. With a mighty voice he shouted:

"Fallen! Fallen is Babylon the Great! She has become a home for demons and a haunt for every evil spirit, a haunt for every unclean and detestable bird. For all the nations have drunk the maddening wine of her adulteries. The kings of the earth committed adultery with her, and the merchants of the earth grew rich from her excessive luxuries."

The downfall and destruction of **Babylon** was an event so fully determined in God's counsels, and of such consequence to his interests and glory, that the visions and predictions about it are repeated.

1. **After this I saw another angel coming down from heaven. He had great authority, and the earth was illuminated by his splendor** (verse 1). Here is **another angel** sent from heaven, who comes with great power and luster. **He had great authority, and the earth was illuminated by his**

splendor. He not only had light in himself to discern the truth of his own prediction, but would inform and enlighten the world about that great event. He not only had light to discern it but the power to accomplish it.

2. This angel spreads the news about the fall of Babylon as something that had already taken place. **With a mighty voice he shouted: "Fallen! Fallen is Babylon the Great! She has become a home for demons and a haunt for every evil spirit, a haunt for every unclean and detestable bird"** (verse 2). He does this with a mighty strong voice—**with a mighty voice he shouted**—so that everyone might hear the cry and see how pleased this angel was to be the messenger of such news. There appears to be an allusion to the prediction of the fall of pagan Babylon here. "'Babylon has fallen, has fallen!'" (Isaiah 21:9). Some people have thought that a double fall is intended here. First her apostasy, and then her ruin. They think the words that follow in the second half of this verse support this: **"She has become a home for demons and a haunt for every evil spirit, a haunt for every unclean and detestable bird."** But this is also borrowed from Isaiah: "'All the images of its gods lie shattered on the ground!'" (Isaiah 21:9). This seems to describe not so much her sin of entertaining idols, which are truly called **demons**, but her punishment. It was a commonly held idea that unclean spirits, as well as ominous and hateful birds, used to haunt a city or the houses that lay in its ruins.

3. The cause of this ruin is declared. Although God is not obliged to give any reason for his actions, he is still pleased to do so. He especially does so in those dispensations of providence that are most awful and tremendous. The wickedness of **Babylon** had been very great, for she had not only forsaken the true God herself and set up idols, but had with great art and industry drawn all sorts of people into spiritual adultery. **"For all the nations have drunk the maddening wine of her adulteries. The kings of the earth committed adultery with her, and the merchants of the earth grew rich from her excessive luxuries"** (verse 3). Through her wealth and **excessive luxuries** she retained her hold over them.

Verses 4-8

Then I heard another voice from heaven say:

"Come out of her, my people, so that you will not share in her sins, so that you will not receive any of her plagues; for her sins are piled up to heaven, and God has remembered her crimes. Give back to her as she has given; pay her back double for what she has done. Mix her a double portion from her own cup. Give her as much torture and grief as the glory and luxury she gave herself. In her heart she boasts, 'I sit as queen; I am not a widow, and I will never mourn.' Therefore in one day her plagues will overtake her: death, mourning and famine. She will be consumed by fire, for mighty is the Lord God who judges her."

Here fair warning is given to all who expect mercy from God, that they should not only **"Come out of her,"** but assist in her destruction. **Then I heard another voice from heaven say: "Come out of her, my people, so that you will not share in her sins, so that you will not receive any of her plagues; for her sins are piled up to heaven, and God has remembered her crimes"** (verses 4-5). Note here:

1. God may have even in **Babylon** people who belong to the election of grace.

2. God's people will be called out of **Babylon,** and called effectually.

3. Those who are resolved to take part with wicked people's sins must receive their plagues.

4. When the sins of a people reach up to heaven, God's wrath reaches down to earth.

5. Though private revenge is forbidden, yet God will have his people act under him, when called to do so, in pulling down his and their inveterate and implacable enemies. **"Give back to her as she has given; pay her back double for what she has done. Mix her a double portion from her own cup"** (verse 6).

6. God will punish sinners according to their wickedness and pride. **"Give her as much torture and grief as the glory and luxury she gave herself. In her heart she boasts, 'I sit as queen; I am not a widow, and I will never mourn'"** (verse 7).

7. When destruction comes on a people suddenly, the surprise is a great aggravation of their misery. **"Therefore in one day her plagues will overtake her: death, mourning and famine. She will be consumed by fire, for mighty is the Lord God who judges her"** (verse 8).

Verses 9-19

"When the kings of the earth who committed adultery with her and shared her luxury see the smoke of her burning, they will weep and mourn over her. Terrified at her torment, they will stand far off and cry:

"'Woe! Woe, O great city, O Babylon, city of power! In one hour your doom has come!'

"The merchants of the earth will weep and mourn over her because no one buys their cargoes any more—cargoes of gold, silver, precious stones and pearls; fine linen, purple, silk and scarlet cloth; every sort of citron wood, and articles of every kind made of ivory, costly wood, bronze, iron and marble; cargoes of cinnamon and spice, of incense, myrrh and frankincense, of wine and olive oil, of fine flour and wheat; cattle and sheep; horses and carriages; and bodies and souls of men.

"They will say, 'The fruit you longed for is gone from you. All your riches and splendor have vanished, never to be recovered.' The merchants who sold these things and gained their wealth from her will

stand far off, terrified at her torment. They will weep and mourn and cry out:

"'Woe! Woe, O great city, dressed in fine linen, purple and scarlet, and glittering with gold, precious stones and pearls! In one hour such great wealth has been brought to ruin!'

"Every sea captain, and all who travel by ship, the sailors, and all who earn their living from the sea, will stand far off. When they see the smoke of her burning, they will exclaim, 'Was there ever a city like this great city?' They will throw dust on their heads, and with weeping and mourning cry out:

"'Woe! Woe, O great city, where all who had ships on the sea became rich through her wealth! In one hour she has been brought to ruin!'"

Here we have a doleful lamentation made by Babylon's friends over her fall. Notice here:

1. Who the mourners are: "When the kings of the earth who committed adultery with her and shared her luxury see the smoke of her burning, they will weep and mourn over her" (verse 9). These are those who had been bewitched by her fornication, those who had shared in her sensual pleasures, and those who had profited from her wealth and trade—the kings of the earth and the merchants of the earth (verse 11). She had flattered these people into idolatry by allowing them to be arbitrary and tyrannical over their subjects while they were fawning before her. The merchants are those who traded in indulgences, pardons, dispensations, and preferments. They will mourn because by this craft they got their wealth.

2. How they mourn:

a. Terrified at her torment, they will stand far off and cry: "Woe! Woe, O great city, O Babylon, city of power! In one hour your doom has come!" (verse 10). They will stand far off, as they did not dare to come close to her. Even Babylon's friends will stand at a distance from her fall. Even though they had taken part in her sins and in her sinful pleasures and activities, they were unwilling to share in her plagues.

b. They make a great cry. "Woe! Woe, O great city, O Babylon, city of power! In one hour your doom has come!"

c. They wept. The merchants of the earth will weep and mourn over her because no one buys their cargoes any more (verse 11). "They will throw dust on their heads, and with weeping and mourning cry out" (18:19). The pleasures of sin only last for "a short time" (see Hebrews 11:25), and then they end in dismal sorrow. All those who rejoice in the success of the church's enemies will share with them in their downfall. Those who have most indulged themselves in pride and pleasure are the least able to bear calamities. Their sorrows will be excessive, as their pleasure and jollity were previously.

3. Why they mourned: it was not because of their sin, but because of

their punishment. They did not weep over their falling into idolatry and luxury and persecution, but over their fall into ruin—the loss of their trade and wealth and power. The spirit of antichrist is a worldly spirit, and their sorrow is a worldly sorrow. They do not lament over God's anger that now fell on them, but over losing their outward comforts— **cargoes of gold, silver, precious stones and pearls; fine linen, purple, silk and scarlet cloth; every sort of citron wood, and articles of every kind made of ivory, costly wood, bronze, iron and marble; cargoes of cinnamon and spice, of incense, myrrh and frankincense, of wine and olive oil, of fine flour and wheat; cattle and sheep; horses and carriages; and bodies and souls of men** (verses 13-14). We have a large schedule and inventory of the wealth and merchandise of this city, all of which was lost, and lost irrecoverably. **They will say, "The fruit you longed for is gone from you. All your riches and splendor have vanished, never to be recovered"** (verse 14). God's church may fall for a time, but she will rise again. But Babylon's fall will be a total overthrow, like that of Sodom and Gomorrah. Godly sorrow is a support under affliction, but mere worldly sorrow adds to the calamity.

Verses 20-24

"'Rejoice over her, O heaven! Rejoice, saints and apostles and prophets! God has judged her for the way she treated you.'"

Then a mighty angel picked up a boulder the size of a large millstone and threw it into the sea, and said:

"With such violence the great city of Babylon will be thrown down, never to be found again. The music of harpists and musicians, flute players and trumpeters, will never be heard in you again. No workman of any trade will ever be found in you again. The sound of a millstone will never be heard in you again. The light of a lamp will never shine in you again. The voice of bridegroom and bride will never be heard in you again. Your merchants were the world's great men. By your magic spell all the nations were led astray. In her was found the blood of prophets and of the saints, and of all who have been killed on the earth."

We have here an account of the joy and triumph both in heaven and on earth at the irrecoverable fall of Babylon. **"Rejoice over her, O heaven! Rejoice, saints and apostles and prophets! God has judged her for the way she treated you"** (verse 20). While her own people were bewailing her, God's servants were called to **"Rejoice over her."** Notice here:

1. How universal this joy would be. Heaven and earth, angels and saints would join in it. What makes God's servants in this world rejoice makes the angels in heaven rejoice as well.

2. This is just and reasonable, for the following reasons:

a. The fall of Babylon was an act of God's vindictive justice. God was avenging his people's cause in this. They had committed their cause to him to whom vengeance belongs, and now the year of recompense was come for the sufferings of Zion. While they did not take pleasure in anyone's miseries, yet they had reason to rejoice in God's glorious justice.

b. Because it was an irrecoverable ruin. The enemy would never again molest them, and they were assured of this by a remarkable token: **Then a mighty angel picked up a boulder the size of a large millstone and threw it into the sea, and said: "With such violence the great city of Babylon will be thrown down, never to be found again"** (verse 21). The place would never be fit to be inhabited again. **The music of harpists and musicians, flute players and trumpeters, will never be heard in you again. No workman of any trade will ever be found in you again. The sound of a millstone will never be heard in you again. The light of a lamp will never shine in you again. The voice of bridegroom and bride will never be heard in you again. Your merchants were the world's great men. By your magic spell all the nations were led astray** (verses 22-23).

No work would be done there, no comfort enjoyed, no light seen, but only utter darkness and desolation, the reward for her great wickedness. **In her was found the blood of prophets and of the saints, and of all who have been killed on the earth** (verse 24). First, because her magic spells had deceived all the nations (see verse 23), and, second, because she had murdered and destroyed those she could not deceive: **in her was found the blood of prophets and of the saints.** Such abominable sins deserved so great a ruin.

Revelation
Chapter 19

Introduction

In this chapter we have:

1. A further account of the triumphant song of the angels and saints concerning the fall of Babylon (verses 1-4).
2. The marriage between Christ and the church proclaimed and perfected (verses 5-10).
3. Another warlike expedition of the glorious Head and Husband of the church, with its success (verses 11-21).

Verses 1-4

After this I heard what sounded like the roar of a great multitude in heaven shouting:

"Hallelujah! Salvation and glory and power belong to our God, for true and just are his judgments. He has condemned the great prostitute who corrupted the earth by her adulteries. He has avenged on her the blood of his servants."

And again they shouted:

"Hallelujah! The smoke from her goes up for ever and ever."

The twenty-four elders and the four living creatures fell down and worshiped God, who was seated on the throne. And they cried:

"Amen, Hallelujah!"

The fall of Babylon had been fixed, finished, and declared irrecoverable in the previous chapter. This chapter begins with a holy triumph over her, following the command given in 18:20: **"Rejoice over her, O heaven! Rejoice, saints and apostles and prophets! God has judged her for the way she treated you."** They now gladly answer this call, and so we have here:

1. The form of their thanksgiving, in that heavenly and most comprehensive word **"Hallelujah!"** They started with this word (verse 1) and they ended with it (verse 4). Their prayers are now turned into praises; their hosannas end in hallelujahs.

2. The content of their thanksgiving: they praise him for the truth of his Word and the righteousness of his providential conduct, especially in this great event—the ruin of **Babylon**. **". . . for true and just are his judgments. He has condemned the great prostitute who corrupted the earth by her adulteries. He has avenged on her the blood of his servants"** (verse 2). **Babylon** had been a mother of idolatry, immorality, and cruelty. For this signal example of divine justice, they ascribe salvation and glory and honor and power to our God.

3. The effect of those praises: when the angels and saints cried, **"Hallelujah!"** Babylon's fire burned more fiercely. **And again they shouted: "Hallelujah! The smoke from her goes up for ever and ever"** (verse 3). The most certain way to have our deliverances continued and completed is to give God the glory for what he has done for us even as we praise God for what we have. This praying is the most effective way to receive what has yet to be done for us. The praises of the saints fuel the fire of God's wrath against the common enemy.

4. The blessed harmony between the angels and the saints in this triumphant song: **The twenty-four elders and the four living creatures fell down and worshiped God, who was seated on the throne. And they cried: "Amen, Hallelujah!"** (verse 4). The churches and their ministers take the melodious sound from the angels and repeat it. Falling down and worshiping God, they cry, **"Amen, Hallelujah!"**

Verses 5-10

Then a voice came from the throne, saying:

"Praise our God, all you his servants, you who fear him, both small and great!"

Then I heard what sounded like a great multitude, like the roar of rushing waters and like loud peals of thunder, shouting:

"Hallelujah! For our Lord God Almighty reigns. Let us rejoice and be glad and give him glory! For the wedding of the Lamb has come, and his bride has made herself ready. Fine linen, bright and clean, was given her to wear."

(Fine linen stands for the righteous acts of the saints.)

Then the angel said to me, "Write: 'Blessed are those who are invited to the wedding supper of the Lamb!'" And he added, "These are the true words of God."

At this I fell at his feet to worship him. But he said to me, "Do not do it! I am a fellow servant with you and with your brothers who hold to the testimony of Jesus. Worship God! For the testimony of Jesus is the spirit of prophecy."

After the triumphant song has ended, a marriage song begins. **Then I heard what sounded like a great multitude, like the roar of rushing waters and like loud peals of thunder, shouting: "Hallelujah! For our Lord God Almighty reigns"** (verse 6). Notice here:

1. The concert of heavenly music. The chorus was large and loud: **like the roar of rushing waters and like loud peals of thunder.** God is fearful in the praises given to him. There is no discord in heaven. The morning stars sing together. There is no jarring string or untuned key, but pure and perfect melody.

2. The occasion of this song: **"Let us rejoice and be glad and give him glory! For the wedding of the Lamb has come, and his bride has made herself ready. Fine linen, bright and clean, was given her to wear"** (verse 7). This was the reign and dominion of that omnipotent God who had redeemed his church by his own blood and is now in a more public manner betrothing her to himself. **"For the wedding of the Lamb has come."** Some think this refers to the conversion of the Jews, which they thought would follow the fall of **Babylon.** Others thought it meant the general resurrection. The former seems more probable. Note:

a. You have here a description of how the bride appeared. She was not dressed in the bright and gaudy attire of the mother of prostitutes, but in **fine linen, bright and clean.** Verse 8 states: **Fine linen stands for the righteous acts of the saints.** She wears the robes of Christ's righteousness, both imputed for justification and imparted for sanctification—the white robe of absolution, adoption, and enfranchisement and the white robe of purity and universal holiness. "They have washed their robes and made them white in the blood of the Lamb" (7:14). She did not buy her nuptial ornaments at any price or on her own but received them as the gift and grant of her blessed Lord.

b. The marriage feast, though not particularly described, as in Matthew 22:4, yet is declared to be such as would make them all happy. **Then the angel said to me, "Write: 'Blessed are those who are invited to the wedding supper of the Lamb!'" And he added, "These are the true words of God"** (verse 9). They are called to this marriage feast, and they accept the invitation to a feast made up of the promises of the Gospel, **the true words of God.** These promises, opened, applied, sealed, and given as a guarantee through the Spirit of God, seen in holy, Eucharistic ordinances, are the marriage feast. The whole collective body of all those who take part in this feast is the bride, the Lamb's wife. They eat one body and drink of one spirit and are not mere spectators or guests. They coalesce into the marriage party, the mystical body of Christ.

c. The joy that the apostle felt in himself at this vision: **At this I fell at his feet to worship him. But he said to me, "Do not do it! I am a fellow** servant with you and with your brothers who hold to the testimony of Jesus. Worship God! For the testimony of Jesus is the spirit of prophecy" (verse 10). He fell at his feet to worship him. John thought the angel was more than a creature, or perhaps he had his thoughts dominated by the strength of his affections. Notice here:

(1) What honor he offered the angel: I fell at his feet to worship him. This prostration was a part of external worship. It was a posture of proper adoration.

(2) How the angel refused it, with some resentment: "Do not do it!" "Think about what you are doing, for you are doing the wrong thing."

(3) The angel gave a very good reason for his refusal: "I am a fellow servant with you and with your brothers who hold to the testimony of Jesus." "I am a creature, your equal in office, though not in nature. I too, as an angel and messenger of God, hold to the testimony of Jesus, to be a witness for him and to testify about him. And you, as an apostle, having the spirit of prophecy, have the same testimony to give. Therefore we are brothers and fellow servants."

(4) He directs John to the true and only object of religious worship: "Worship God!" That is, "Worship *only* God." This completely condemns the practice both of the papists in worshiping the elements of bread and wine and saints and angels, and the practice of the Socinians and Arians, who do not believe Christ is truly and by nature God and yet pay him religious worship. This shows what wretched fig leaves all their evasions and excuses offer in their own vindication. They stand thereby convicted of idolatry by a messenger from heaven.

Verses 11-21

I saw heaven standing open and there before me was a white horse, whose rider is called Faithful and True. With justice he judges and makes war. His eyes are like blazing fire, and on his head are many crowns. He has a name written on him that no one but he himself knows. He is dressed in a robe dipped in blood, and his name is the Word of God. The armies of heaven were following him, riding on white horses and dressed in fine linen, white and clean. Out of his mouth comes a sharp sword with which to strike down the nations. "He will rule them with an iron scepter." He treads the winepress of the fury of the wrath of God Almighty. On his robe and on his thigh he has this name written:

KING OF KINGS AND LORD OF LORDS.

And I saw an angel standing in the sun, who cried in a loud voice to all the birds flying in midair, "Come, gather together for the great supper of God, so that you may eat the flesh of kings, generals, and mighty men, of horses and their riders, and the flesh of all people, free and slave, small and great."

Then I saw the beast and the kings of the earth and their armies gathered together to make war against the rider on the horse and his army. But the beast was captured, and with him the false prophet who had performed the miraculous signs on his behalf. With these signs he had deluded those who had received the mark of the beast and worshiped his image. The two of them were thrown alive into the fiery lake of burning sulfur. The rest of them were killed with the sword that came out of the mouth of the rider on the horse, and all the birds gorged themselves on their flesh.

No sooner is the marriage solemnized between Christ and his church by the conversion of the Jews than the glorious Head and Husband of the church is called out on a new expedition. This seems to be the great battle that was to be fought at Armageddon, as was foretold: "Then they gathered the kings together to the place that in Hebrew is called Armageddon" (16:16). Observe here:

1. The description of the Commander: **I saw heaven standing open and there before me was a white horse, whose rider is called Faithful and True. With justice he judges and makes war** (verse 1).

a. The center of his empire: **heaven.** His throne is there, and his power and authority are heavenly and divine.

b. His equipment: he is again described as sitting on **a white horse,** to show the justice of his cause and its certain success.

c. His attributes: he is **called Faithful and True** to his covenant and promise. **With justice** he carries out all his military maneuvers. **His eyes are like blazing fire, and on his head are many crowns. He has a name written on him that no one but he himself knows** (verse 12). He has penetrating insight into all the strength and stratagems of his enemies: **his eyes are like blazing fire.** He has a large and extensive dominion: **on his head are many crowns,** for he is **KING OF KINGS AND LORD OF LORDS** (verse 16).

d. His armor: **He is dressed in a robe dipped in blood, and his name is the Word of God** (verse 13). **He is dressed in a robe dipped in blood.** This is either his own blood, through which he purchased this mediatorial power, or the blood of his enemies, over whom he has always prevailed.

e. His name: **His name is the Word of God.** He has a name that nobody fully understands except himself. We know that "the Word became flesh and lived for a while among us" (John 1:14), but his perfections are not able to be understood by anyone.

2. The army that he commands: **The armies of heaven were following him, riding on white horses and dressed in fine linen, white and clean** (verse 14). This is a very large force, made up of many **armies.** Angels and

saints followed Christ's command and copied him in their equipment, the armor of purity and righteousness; they were chosen, called, and faithful.

3. The weapons of his warfare. **Out of his mouth comes a sharp sword with which to strike down the nations. "He will rule them with an iron scepter." He treads the winepress of the fury of the wrath of God Almighty"** (verse 15). **Out of his mouth comes a sharp sword.** He uses this sword to **strike down the nations.** This means either the threats of the written Word, which he is now going to carry out, or more probably his word of command, calling on his followers to take just revenge on his and their enemies who are now put into **the winepress of the fury of the wrath of God Almighty.**

4. The ensigns of his authority, his coat of arms: **On his robe and on his thigh he has this name written: KING OF KINGS AND LORD OF LORDS** (verse 16). This asserts his authority and power, and the cause he is fighting for.

5. **And I saw an angel standing in the sun, who cried in a loud voice to all the birds flying in midair, "Come, gather together for the great supper of God, so that you may eat the flesh of kings, generals, and mighty men, of horses and their riders, and the flesh of all people, free and slave, small and great"** (verses 17-18). An invitation is given to **the birds flying in midair** (verse 17) to come and see the battle and share in the spoil and pillage of the field. This intimates that this great decisive engagement should leave the enemies of the church a feast for the birds of prey, and that all the world would have good reason to rejoice in the result of the battle.

6. The battle starts, and the enemy attacks with great fury. **Then I saw the beast and the kings of the earth and their armies gathered together to make war against the rider on the horse and his army** (verse 19). The enemies' leaders were **the beast and the kings of the earth.** The powers of earth and hell **gathered together to make war** and brought all their strength into the battle.

7. The victory won by the great and glorious Head of the church: **But the beast was captured, and with him the false prophet who had performed the miraculous signs on his behalf. With these signs he had deluded those who had received the mark of the beast and worshiped his image. The two of them were thrown alive into the fiery lake of burning sulfur** (verse 20). **The beast . . . and . . . the false prophet,** the leaders of the army, were taken prisoners, both he who led them by power and he who led them by action and falsehood. **The two of them were thrown alive into the fiery lake of burning sulfur.** They were rendered incapable of ever hurting God's church again.

The rest of them were killed with the sword that came out of the mouth of the rider on the horse, and all the birds gorged themselves on their flesh (verse 21). Their followers, whether officers or common soldiers, are given up to military execution and are made a feast for **all the birds.** Although the divine vengeance will mainly fall on the beast and the false prophet, there will be no excuse for those who fought under their banner, followed their leadership, and obeyed their commands. As they had decided to fight for them, they must fall and perish with them. "Therefore, you kings, be wise; be warned, you rulers of the earth. . . . Kiss the Son, lest he be angry and you be destroyed in your way" (Psalm 2:10, 12).

Revelation
Chapter 20

Introduction

Some people think this chapter is the darkest part of this book of prophecy. It is very probable that the things that it mentions have not yet been accomplished. Therefore, it is best to content ourselves with general observations rather than particular ones in our explanations. Here we have an account of:

1. The binding of Satan for 1,000 years (verses 1-3).
2. The reign of the saints with Christ for the same length of time (verses 4-6).
3. The loosing of Satan, and the conflict of the church with Gog and Magog (verses 7-10).
4. The day of judgment (verses 11-15).

Verses 1-3

And I saw an angel coming down out of heaven, having the key to the Abyss and holding in his hand a great chain. He seized the dragon, that ancient serpent, who is the devil, or Satan, and bound him for a thousand years. He threw him into the Abyss, and locked and sealed it over him, to keep him from deceiving the nations any more until the thousand years were ended. After that, he must be set free for a short time.

We have here a prophecy about the binding of Satan for a certain length of time, during which he would have much less power, and the church much more peace, than before. The power of Satan was partly broken when the gospel-kingdom was set up in the world and was further weakened when the empire became Christian, and was additionally weakened with the downfall of the mystical Babylon. But this serpent still had many heads, and when one was wounded, another still had life in it. Here we have a further limitation or reduction of his power. So note here:

1. To whom this work of binding Satan is committed: to **an angel coming down out of heaven** (verse 1). It is most likely that this angel is none other than the Lord Jesus Christ. His description fits no one else. **He seized the dragon, that ancient serpent, who is the devil, or Satan, and bound him for a thousand years** (verse 2). He is the one who has the power to bind the strong armed man, to cast him out, and to spoil his goods.

2. The means he uses in this work: he has **a great chain** to bind Satan and **the key** to the prison in which he was to be confined. Christ never lacks the necessary powers and instruments to break the power of Satan, for he holds the powers of heaven and the keys of hell. Note further:

a. The carrying out of his work: **He seized the dragon, that ancient serpent, who is the devil, or Satan.** Neither the strength of the dragon, nor the subtlety of the serpent was enough to deliver him out of Christ's hands. Christ caught hold of the devil, and kept hold of him.

b. **He threw him into the Abyss, and locked and sealed it over him, to keep him from deceiving the nations any more until the thousand years were ended. After that, he must be set free for a short time** (verse 3). **He threw him into the Abyss.** He threw him down with force, and with just vengeance, to his own place and prison after he had been permitted to disturb the churches and deceive the nations. Now he is kept there in chains.

c. He **locked and sealed it over him.** Christ shuts, and no one can open. He shuts by his power and seals by his authority. And his lock and seal, even the devil cannot break open.

d. We have here the length of Satan's imprisonment—a **thousand years.** After this he would **be set free for a short time.** The church would have a considerable time of peace and prosperity, but all her trials were not yet over.

Verses 4-6

I saw thrones on which were seated those who had been given author-ity to judge. And I saw the souls of those who had been beheaded because of their testimony for Jesus and because of the word of God. They had not worshiped the beast or his image and had not received his mark on their foreheads or their hands. They came to life and reigned with Christ a thousand years. (The rest of the dead did not come to life until the thousand years were ended.) This is the first resurrection. Blessed and holy are those who have part in the first resurrection. The second death has no power over them, but they will be priests of God and of Christ and will reign with him for a thousand years.

We have here an account of the rule of the saints for the same length of time in which Satan continues to be bound. Note here:

1. Who they were that received such honor: **I saw thrones on which were seated those who had been given authority to judge. And I saw the souls of those who had been beheaded because of their testimony for Jesus and because of the word of God. They had not worshiped the beast or his image and had not received his mark on their foreheads or their hands. They came to life and reigned with Christ for a thousand years** (verse 4). Those who were honored were those who had suffered for Christ, all those who had faithfully followed him and who **had not received his**—that is, the beast's—**mark on their foreheads or their hands.** These were those who **had not worshiped the beast or his image**, all those who had kept themselves clear of pagan and papal idolatry.

2. The honor bestowed on them:

a. They were raised from the dead and restored to life. **They came to life.** This may be taken either literally or figuratively. They were in a civil and political sense dead and had a political resurrection. Their freedom and privileges were revived and restored.

b. Thrones and the power of judgment were given to them. They possessed great honor and authority. I think this was of a spiritual nature rather than a secular one.

c. They **reigned with Christ a thousand years.** "Now if we are children, then we are heirs—heirs of God and co-heirs with Christ, if indeed we share in his sufferings in order that we may also share in his glory" (Romans 8:17). They will reign with him in his spiritual and heavenly kingdom, in glorious conformity to him in wisdom, righteousness, and holiness, beyond what had been known before in the world. **(The rest of the dead did not come to life until the thousand years were ended.) This is the first resurrection. Blessed and holy are those who have part in the first resurrection. The second death has no power over them, but they will be priests of God and of Christ and will reign with him for a thousand years** (verses 5-6). This is called **the first resurrection** (verse 6). Nobody other than those who have served Christ and suffered for him will be favored with this. As for the wicked, they will not be raised up and restored to their power again until Satan is let loose. This may be called a "resurrection" just as the conversion of the Jews is said to be "life from the dead."

3. The happiness of these servants of God is declared.

a. They are **blessed and holy** (verse 6). All who are **holy** will be **blessed.** These people were **holy** as a sort of firstfruits to God in this spiritual resurrection, and as such were **blessed** by him.

b. They were delivered from the power of **the second death** (verse 6). This is a much more dreadful death than the first death, for it is the death of the soul, eternal separation from God. The Lord grant that we may never know what this is by experience. Those who have had an experience of a spiritual resurrection are saved from the **power** of **the second death** (verse 6).

Verses 7-10

When the thousand years are over, Satan will be released from his prison and will go out to deceive the nations in the four corners of the earth—Gog and Magog—to gather them for battle. In number they are like the sand on the seashore. They marched across the breadth of the earth and surrounded the camp of God's people, the city he loves. But fire came down from heaven and devoured them. And the devil, who deceived them, was thrown into the lake of burning sulfur, where the beast and the false prophet had been thrown. They will be tormented day and night for ever and ever.

Here we have an account of the return of the church's troubles, and another mighty conflict, very sharp but short and decisive. Notice:

1. The restraints laid for a long time on Satan are at length taken off: **When the thousand years are over, Satan will be released from his prison** (verse 7). While the world lasts, Satan's power in it will not be wholly destroyed. It may be limited and lessened, but he will still disturb God's people.

2. No sooner is Satan let loose than he carries on his old work: **. . . and will go out to deceive the nations in the four corners of the earth—Gog and Magog—to gather them for battle. In number they are like the sand on the seashore** (verse 8). He **will go out to deceive the nations,** and so stir them up to make war against the saints and servants of God, which they would never do if they had not been deceived in the first place. They are deceived on two counts. They are deceived about the cause they engage in. They believe it is a good cause when it is indeed a very bad one. And they are deceived about the result of the cause. They expect to be successful but are sure to lose the day.

3. Satan's last efforts seem to be the greatest. The power he is now allowed seems even more unlimited than before. He now has freedom to enlist his volunteers from **the four corners of the earth.** He has raised an army **in number . . . like the sand of the seashore.**

4. We are given the names of the leading commanders in this army under the dragon—**Gog and Magog.** We should not be too inquisitive about the particular powers that are meant by these names, since the army was gathered from all parts of the world. These names are found in other parts of Scripture. **Magog** comes in Genesis: "The sons of Japheth: Gomer, Magog, Madai, Javan, Tubal, Meshech and Tiras" (10:2). He was one of the sons of Japheth and lived in a country called Syria, from where his descendants spread into many other parts. Gog and Magog are only

mentioned together in one other place. "Son of man, set your face against Gog, of the land of Magog, the chief prince of Meshech and Tubal" (Ezekiel 38:2). Revelation borrows many of its images from the prophetic book of Ezekiel.

5. We have the march and military disposition of this formidable army: **They marched across the breadth of the earth and surrounded the camp of God's people, the city he loves** (verse 9). **The city he loves** is spiritual Jerusalem, in which the most precious interests of the people of God are centered, and therefore to them is a beloved city. The army of the saints is described as being drawn from the city and lying under its walls to defend it. They were encamped around Jerusalem. But the enemy's army was far superior to the church's army, and they surrounded them and their city.

6. We have an account of the battle and the result of this war: **Fire came down from heaven and devoured them.** Thus the ruin of Gog and Magog is foretold: "I will summon a sword against Gog on all my mountains, declares the Sovereign LORD. Every man's sword will be against his brother. I will execute judgment upon him with plague and bloodshed; I will pour down torrents of rain, hailstones and burning sulfur on him and on his troops and on the many nations with him" (Ezekiel 38:21-22). God would in an extraordinary and more immediate manner fight this last and decisive battle for his people, that the victory might be complete, and the glory redound to himself.

7. The doom and punishment of the great enemy: **the devil, who deceived them, was thrown into the lake of burning sulfur, where the beast and the false prophet had been thrown. They will be tormented day and night for ever and ever** (verse 10). **The devil** is now **thrown into** hell, along with his two great officers, **the beast and the false prophet**, tyranny and idolatry. They were not thrown there for any limited length of time but will **be tormented day and night for ever and ever.**

Verses 11-15

Then I saw a great white throne and him who was seated on it. Earth and sky fled from his presence, and there was no place for them. And I saw the dead, great and small, standing before the throne, and books were opened. Another book was opened, which is the book of life. The dead were judged according to what they had done as recorded in the books. The sea gave up the dead that were in it, and death and Hades gave up the dead that were in them, and each person was judged according to what he had done. Then death and Hades were thrown into the lake of fire. The lake of fire is the second death. If anyone's name was not found written in the book of life, he was thrown into the lake of fire.

The utter destruction of the devil's kingdom quite correctly leads to an account of the day of judgment, which will determine every person's everlasting state. We can be quite certain that there will be a judgment and that the prince of this world will be judged. "When he [the Counselor, the Holy Spirit] comes, he will convict the world of . . . judgment. . . . because the prince of this world now stands condemned" (John 16:8, 11). "For we will all stand before God's judgment seat" (Romans 14:10). "For we must all appear before the judgment seat of Christ, that each one may receive what is due him for the things done while in the body, whether good or bad" (2 Corinthians 5:10). May the Lord help us firmly to believe this doctrine of the judgment to come. It is a doctrine that made Felix tremble. "As Paul discoursed on righteousness, self-control and the judgment to come, Felix was afraid" (Acts 24:25). Here we have this coming judgment described. So notice:

1. **Then I saw a great white throne and him who was seated on it. Earth and sky fled from his presence, and there was no place for them** (verse 11). We see **a great white throne.** This is the tribunal of judgment, **great** and **white,** very glorious, perfectly just and righteous. "Can a corrupt throne be allied with you—one that brings on misery by its decrees?" (Psalm 94:20). A corrupt throne has no fellowship with this righteous throne and tribunal.

2. The appearance of the Judge, that is, the Lord Jesus Christ, who then put on such majesty and terror that **earth and sky fled from his presence, and there was no place for them.** There will be a dissolution of the whole frame of nature. "But the day of the Lord will come like a thief. The heavens will disappear with a roar; the elements will be destroyed by fire, and the earth and everything in it will be laid bare" (2 Peter 3:10).

3. The people to be judged. **And I saw the dead, great and small, standing before the throne, and books were opened. Another book was opened, which is the book of life. The dead were judged according to what they had done as recorded in the books** (verse 12). **The dead, great and small.** Both young and old, low and high, poor and rich—everyone must give an account. Nobody is so great that he or she can avoid the jurisdiction of this court. Not only those people who are still alive at Christ's coming, but all who have died before that time will appear. The grave will give up the bodies of people, hell will surrender the souls of the wicked, and the sea will surrender the many who seemed to have been lost in it. **The sea gave up the dead that were in it, and death and Hades gave up the dead that were in them, and each person was judged according to what he had done** (verse 14). All these realms are the King's prisons, and he will make them bring out their prisoners.

4. The rule of judgment is settled. **Books were opened** (verse 12). What books? The book of the omniscience of God, who is greater than our consciences and knows all things. There is a book of remembrance with him

both for good and bad. Also the book of the sinner's conscience, which though previously secret will now be opened. Yet **another book was opened, which is the book of life** (verse 12). This is the book of the Scriptures, the statute book of heaven, the rule of life. This contains the law, the touchstone by which the hearts and lives of people are tried. This book determines matters of right and wrong; the other books give evidence about matters of fact. Some people think this other book, called **the book of life,** is the book of God's eternal counsels. But that does not seem to fit in with the theme of judgment. In eternal election God does not act judicially but with absolute, sovereign freedom.

5. The cause to be tried: the deeds of men. By their deeds people are either justified or condemned. **Each person was judged according to what he had done** (verse 13). God knows people's principles, and he looks mainly at these. But he shows himself to be a righteous God, both to angels and to humans, and so he tests people's principles by their practices, and so will be just when he speaks.

6. The result of the trial and judgment. This will be according to the evidence of the facts and the rule of judgment. **Then death and Hades were thrown into the lake of fire. The lake of fire is the second death** (verse 14). Everyone who has a covenant with death and an agreement with hell will be condemned with their infernal confederates and thrown with them into **the lake of fire.** They are not entitled to eternal life, according to the rules of life laid down in Scripture.

If anyone's name was not found written in the book of life, he was thrown into the lake of fire (verse 15). Those people whose names are written in **the book of life**—that is, those who are justified and acquitted by the Gospel—will be justified and acquitted by the Judge and will enter into eternal life, having nothing more to fear from death or hell or wicked men, for they are all destroyed together. Let it be our great concern to see on what terms we stand with our Bibles, whether they justify us or condemn us, for the Judge of all will proceed by that rule. "God will judge men's secrets through Jesus Christ" (Romans 2:16). Happy are those who have so ordered and stated their cause according to the Gospel as to know beforehand that they will be justified in the great day of the Lord!

Revelation
Chapter 21

Introduction

Until now the prophecy of this book has presented us with a very remarkable mixture of light and shade, prosperity and adversity, mercy and judgment in the conduct of divine providence toward the church in the world.
Now, at the close of everything, the day breaks, and the shadows flee
away, and a new world appears, for the former one has passed away. Some
are willing to understand all that is said in these last two chapters to be
about the state of the church here on earth, in the glory of the latter days.
But others, more plausibly, take it to represent the perfect and triumphant
state of the church in heaven. Let but the faithful saints and servants of
God wait a while, and they shall not only see but enjoy the perfect holiness and happiness of that world. In this chapter we have:

1. An introduction to the vision of new Jerusalem (verses 1-9).
2. The vision itself (verses 10-27).

Verses 1-8

Then I saw a new heaven and a new earth, for the first heaven and the
first earth had passed away, and there was no longer any sea. I saw the
Holy City, the new Jerusalem, coming down out of heaven from God,
prepared as a bride beautifully dressed for her husband. And I heard a
loud voice from the throne saying, "Now the dwelling of God is with
men, and he will live with them. They will be his people, and God himself will be with them and be their God. He will wipe every tear from
their eyes. There will be no more death or mourning or crying or pain,
for the old order of things has passed away."
He who was seated on the throne said, "I am making everything

new!" Then he said, "Write this down, for these words are trustworthy and true."

He said to me: "It is done. I am the Alpha and the Omega, the Beginning and the End. To him who is thirsty I will give to drink without cost from the spring of the water of life. He who overcomes will inherit all this, and I will be his God and he will be my son. But the cowardly, the unbelieving, the vile, the murderers, the sexually immoral, those who practice magic arts, the idolaters and all liars—their place will be in the fiery lake of burning sulfur. This is the second death."

We have here a more general account of the happiness of the church of God in the future state, by which it seems most safe to understand the heavenly state.

1. A new world now opens to our view: **Then I saw a new heaven and a new earth, for the first heaven and the first earth had passed away, and there was no longer any sea** (verse 1). **I saw a new heaven and a new earth**—that is, a new universe, for we suppose that the world is made up of heaven and earth. By **new earth** we may understand a new state for the bodies of men as well as a **heaven** for their souls. This world is not newly created but newly opened, and is filled with all who are its heirs. The **new heaven and . . . new earth** will not then be distinct. The very earth of the saints, their glorified bodies, will now be spiritual and heavenly and suited to those pure and bright mansions. To make way for the beginning of this new world, the old world, with all its problems and commotions, has **passed away.**

2. **I saw the Holy City, the new Jerusalem, coming down out of heaven from God, prepared as a bride beautifully dressed for her husband** (verse 2). In this new world the apostle **saw the Holy City, the new Jerusalem, coming down out of heaven,** not in regard to its location but to its origin. This **new Jerusalem** is the church of God in its new and perfect state, **prepared as a bride beautifully dressed for her husband.** The church is beautified with all perfection of wisdom and holiness, fit for the full fruition of the Lord Jesus Christ in glory.

3. The blessed presence of God with his people is here proclaimed and admired. **And I heard a loud voice from the throne saying, "Now the dwelling of God is with men, and he will live with them. They will be his people, and God himself will be with them and be their God"** (verse 3). Notice:

a. The presence of God with his church is the glory of the church.

b. It is a matter of wonder that a holy God should ever live with any of the children of men.

c. The presence of God with his people in heaven will not be interrupted as it is on earth, but he will live with them continually.

4. The covenant, interest, and relation that now exist between God and

his people will be completed and perfected in heaven: **They will be his people.** Their souls will be in indissoluble union with him, filled with all the love, honor, and delight in God that their relationship to him requires. This will be their perfect holiness, and **God himself will be with them and be their God.** His immediate presence with them, his love fully manifested to them, and his glory put on them will be their perfect happiness. He will fully answer the character of the relationship on his part, as they will do on their part.

5. This new and blessed state will be free from all trouble and sorrow. For:

a. All the effects of former trouble will be done away with. **He will wipe every tear from their eyes. There will be no more death or mourning or crying or pain, for the old order of things has passed away** (verse 4). They were previously often crying because of sin, affliction, or the calamities of the church. But now he wipes **every tear from their eyes.** No remembrance of former sorrows will remain except to make their present happiness the greater. God himself, as their tender Father, with his kind hand **will wipe every tear** from his children's eyes.

b. All the causes of sorrow will be forever removed. **There will be no more death . . . or pain.** Therefore there will be no **mourning or crying.** Such things belonged to their previous state, but now this **order of things has passed away.**

6. The truth and certainty of this blessed state are ratified by the word and promise of God and are ordered to be committed to writing, as a perpetual record: **He who was seated on the throne said, "I am making everything new!" Then he said, "Write this down, for these words are trustworthy and true"** (verse 5). The subject matter of this vision is so great and of such great importance to the church and people of God that they require the fullest assurances about it. So God, from heaven, repeats and ratifies the truth about this. Besides, many ages would pass between the time this vision was given and its fulfillment. Many great trials would occur in the intervening time. Therefore, God wanted it committed to writing, so it could always be remembered and be of continuing use to his people. Notice:

a. The certainty of the promise asserted: **"these words are trustworthy and true."** This is followed by: **He said to me: "It is done. I am the Alpha and the Omega, the Beginning and the End. To him who is thirsty I will give to drink without cost from the spring of the water of life"** (verse 6). **"It is done."** This is saying that it is as certain as if it had already happened. We may and ought to take God's promise as present payment. If he has said, **"I am making everything new"** (verse 5), **"it is done."**

b. He gives us his titles of honor as a pledge or surety of the full performance. These titles are: **"I am the Alpha and the Omega, the**

Beginning and the End." As it was his glory to give the rise and beginning to the world and to his church, it will be his glory to finish the work begun, and not to leave it imperfect. As his power and will were the first cause of all things, his pleasure and glory are the goal, and he will not fail in his purposes, for then he would no longer be **the Alpha and the Omega.** Men may start projects they never complete, but the counsel of God will stand, and he will do all his pleasure.

c. The desires of his people toward this blessed state are further evidence of its truth and certainty. They thirst after a state of sinless perfection and the uninterrupted enjoyment of God. And God has placed in them these longings that cannot be satisfied with anything else. They would torment the soul if they were disappointed. But it would be inconsistent with God's goodness and the love he has for his people to create in them holy and heavenly desires, and then deny them their proper satisfaction. So they may be assured, when they have overcome their present difficulties, that he **"will give to drink without cost from the spring of the water of life."**

7. The greatness of this future happiness is declared and illustrated:

a. By its freeness. It is the free gift of God. He gives **"to drink without cost."** This will not make his people less grateful, but more.

b. By its fullness. **"He who overcomes will inherit all this, and I will be his God and he will be my son"** (verse 7). God's people then lie at the fountainhead of all blessedness: they **inherit all this.** Enjoying God, they enjoy all things. He is all in all.

c. By the tenure and title by which they enjoy this blessedness—the right of inheritance: **"he will be my son."** They are sons of God. This is the most honorable of all titles, resulting from such a close and affectionate relationship with God himself. It can no more cease to exist than the relationship from which it stems can end.

d. By the completely different state of the wicked. Their misery helps to illustrate the blessedness and glory of the saints, and the special goodness of God toward them. **"But the cowardly, the unbelieving, the vile, the murderers, the sexually immoral, those who practice magic arts, the idolaters and all liars—their place will be in the fiery lake of burning sulfur. This is the second death"** (verse 8). Note here:

(1) The sins of those who perish. They are **cowardly** and **unbelieving.** The **cowardly** head this dark list. They do not dare to encounter the difficulties of religion, and their slavish fear stems from their unbelief. Those who are so contemptuous as not to take up the cross of Christ and carry out their duty toward him are so desperate that they sink into all kinds of abominable wickedness—murder, immorality, **magic arts,** idolatry, and lying.

(2) Their punishment. **"Their place will be in the fiery lake of burning sulfur. This is the second death."** They would not burn at a stake for

Christ, but they must burn in hell for sin. Second, they must die another death after their natural death. The agonies and terrors of the first death will consign them over to the far greater terrors and agonies of eternal death, where they will die and will always be dying. Third, this misery will be their proper portion, what they have justly deserved, what they have in effect chosen, and what they have prepared themselves for by their sins. Thus the misery of the damned will illustrate the blessedness of those who are saved, and the blessedness of the saved will aggravate the misery of those who are damned.

Verses 9-21

One of the seven angels who had the seven bowls full of the seven last plagues came and said to me, "Come, I will show you the bride, the wife of the Lamb." And he carried me away in the Spirit to a mountain great and high, and showed me the Holy City, Jerusalem, coming down out of heaven from God. It shone with the glory of God, and its brilliance was like that of a very precious jewel, like a jasper, clear as crystal. It had a great, high wall with twelve gates, and with twelve angels at the gates. On the gates were written the names of the twelve tribes of Israel. There were three gates on the east, three on the north, three on the south and three on the west. The wall of the city had twelve foundations, and on them were the names of the twelve apostles of the Lamb.

The angel who talked with me had a measuring rod of gold to measure the city, its gates and its wall. The city was laid out like a square, as long as it was wide. He measured the city with the rod and found it to be 12,000 stadia in length, and as wide and high as it is long. He measured its wall and it was 144 cubits thick, by man's measurement, which the angel was using. The wall was made of jasper, and the city of pure gold, as pure as glass. The foundations of the city walls were decorated with every kind of precious stone. The first foundation was jasper, the second sapphire, the third chalcedony, the fourth emerald, the fifth sardonyx, the sixth carnelian, the seventh chrysolite, the eighth beryl, the ninth topaz, the tenth chrysoprase, the eleventh jacinth, and the twelfth amethyst. The twelve gates were twelve pearls, each gate made of a single pearl. The street of the city was of pure gold, like transparent glass.

We have already considered the introduction to the vision of the new Jerusalem in a general way, as the heavenly state. We come now to the vision itself. Here we note:

1. The person who opened the vision to the apostle: **One of the seven angels who had the seven bowls full of the seven last plagues came and said to me, "Come, I will show you the bride, the wife of the Lamb"**

179

(verse 9). **One of the seven angels.** God has a variety of work and use for his angels. Sometimes they have to sound the trumpet of divine providence and give fair warning to a careless world; sometimes they have to pour out the bowls of God's anger on impenitent sinners; and sometimes they discover things of a heavenly nature for those who are heirs of salvation. They readily execute every commission God gives them. When this world comes to an end, the angels will be used by the great God in proper, pleasant work for all eternity.

2. The place from which the apostle had this glorious view: **And he carried me away in the Spirit to a mountain great and high, and showed me the Holy City, Jerusalem, coming down out of heaven from God** (verse 10). **A mountain great and high.** He was in ecstasy on a high mountain. From such vantage points men usually have the most clear view of neighboring cities. People who want clear views of heaven must come as close to heaven as they can, on the mount of vision, the mount of meditation and faith, from where, as from Pisgah, they may view the goodly land of the heavenly Canaan. "Go up to the top of Pisgah and look west and north and south and east. Look at the land with your own eyes" (Deuteronomy 3:27).

3. The subject matter of the vision: the **bride**, the Lamb's **wife** (verse 9)—that is, God's church in her glorious, perfect, triumphant state, under the resemblance of Jerusalem. Jerusalem had the glory of God shining in it. The bride shone because of the brightness of her Husband. The church is glorious in her relationship to Christ. His image is now perfected in her and in his favor shining on her.

Now we have a long description of the triumphant church under the emblem of a city that far exceeds the riches and splendor of all the cities in this world. This **Holy City, Jerusalem** is portrayed before us, both its inside and its exterior.

a. The exterior of the city—the wall and the gates. The wall was for security, and the gates were the points of entry.

(1) The wall for security. **He measured its wall and it was 144 cubits thick, by man's measurement, which the angel was using** (verse 17). Heaven is a safe state. Those who are in heaven are enclosed by a wall that separates them from all evils and enemies. Here is a description of the wall, where we note:

First, its height. We are told it is very high, **12,000 stadia** (verse 16). This was sufficient for ornament and for security.

Second, what it was made of: **The wall was made of jasper** (verse 18). This wall was built of the most precious stones, for strength and for brightness. **It shone with the glory of God, and its brilliance was like that of a very precious jewel, like a jasper, clear as crystal** (verse 11). This city has a wall that is impregnable as well as precious.

Third, the wall's form was very regular and uniform. **The city was laid** out like a square, as long as it was wide (verse 16). In the new Jerusalem everything will be equal in purity and perfection. There will be complete uniformity in the church triumphant. This is lacking and longed for on earth, and is not to be expected until we come to heaven.

Fourth, the length of the wall. **The angel who talked with me had a measuring rod of gold to measure the city, its gates and its wall. The city was laid out like a square, as long as it is wide. He measured the city with the rod and found it to be 12,000 stadia in length, and as wide and high as it was long** (verses 15-16). It measured **12,000 stadia** each way, on each side. This is 1,400 miles. Here there is enough room for all of God's people. "In my Father's house are many rooms" (John 14:2).

Fifth, the foundation of the wall. Heaven is a city that has foundations. **The foundations of the city walls were decorated with every kind of precious stone** (verse 19). The promise and power of God and the purchase of Christ are the strong foundations of the church's happiness and safety. The number of foundations and what they were made of are described. **The wall of the city had twelve foundations, and on them were the names of the twelve apostles of the Lamb** (verse 14). There were **twelve foundations**, alluding to the **twelve apostles.** The apostles' gospel-doctrines are the foundations on which the church is built, but Christ is the chief cornerstone. "You are . . . built on the foundation of the apostles and prophets, with Christ Jesus himself as the chief cornerstone" (Ephesians 2:19-20). As far as the makeup of the foundations is concerned, they are composed of various and precious materials, with twelve kinds of precious stones, denoting the variety and excellency of the doctrines of the Gospel, or the graces of the Holy Spirit, or the personal excellencies of the Lord Jesus Christ.

(2) The gates to enter through. Heaven is not inaccessible. There is a way opened to the holiest of all. There is free admission to those who are sanctified. They will not find themselves shut out. Notice concerning these gates:

First, their number. **It had a great, high wall with twelve gates, and with twelve angels at the gates. On the gates were written the names of the twelve tribes of Israel** (verse 12). There were **twelve gates**, representing **the twelve tribes of Israel.** All the true Israel of God will have entry into the new Jerusalem, just as every tribe had entry into earthly Jerusalem.

Second, the guards that were placed on them. The guards were **twelve angels.** They admitted and received the various tribes of the spiritual Israel and kept other people out.

Third, the inscription on the gates. **On the gates were written the names of the twelve tribes of Israel.** The names of the twelve tribes of Israel show they have a right to the tree of life and to enter through the gates of the city.

Fourth, the location of the gates. As the city had four equal sides, mirroring the four quarters of the world—east, west, north, and south—so on each side there were three gates, symbolizing that from all quarters of the earth people will come who will arrive safely in heaven and be received there, and that there is free entry from one part of the world as much as from another. "Here there is no Greek or Jew, circumcised or uncircumcised, barbarian, Scythian, slave or free, but Christ is all, and is in all" (Colossians 3:11). People from all nations and languages who believe on Christ have access to God through him by grace here on earth and in glory hereafter.

Fifth, what these gates are made of. **The twelve gates were twelve pearls, each gate made of a single pearl** (verse 21). They were all pearls, and yet there was variety, for each gate was made of **a single pearl,** either one single pearl of vast size or one single sort of pearl. Christ is the Pearl of great price, and he is our way to God. There is nothing magnificent enough in this world fully to set forth the glory of heaven. Could we through a strong imagination contemplate such a city as is here described, with such a wall and such gates, how amazing, how glorious it would be. And yet this is but a faint and dim representation of what heaven is.

Verses 22-27

I did not see a temple in the city, because the Lord God Almighty and the Lamb are its temple. The city does not need the sun or the moon to shine on it, for the glory of God gives it light, and the Lamb is its lamp. The nations will walk by its light, and the kings of the earth will bring their splendor into it. On no day will its gates ever be shut, for there will be no night there. The glory and honor of the nations will be brought into it. Nothing impure will ever enter it, nor will anyone who does what is shameful or deceitful, but only those whose names are written in the Lamb's book of life.

Now we come to view the interior of the new Jerusalem. We have seen its strong wall and stately gates and glorious guards. Now we are going to be led through the gates into the city itself. The first thing we notice there is its street. **The street of the city was of pure gold, like transparent glass** (verse 21). The saints in heaven tread on gold. The new Jerusalem has several streets. There is the most exact order in heaven. Every saint has his correct room. There is conversation and interaction in heaven as well. The saints are at rest in heaven, but this is no passive rest. It is not a state of sleep and inactivity, but a state of delightful motion. **The nations will walk by its light, and the kings of the earth will bring their splendor into it** (verse 24). They walk with Christ in white. They have communion not only with God but with each other. And all their steps are firm and clean, for the streets they walk upon are pure and clear **gold, like transparent glass** (verse 21).

1. The new Jerusalem, which has no physical temple made by men's hands like Solomon's or Zerubbabel's, does have a completely spiritual and divine temple. **I did not see a temple in the city, because the Lord God Almighty and the Lamb are its temple** (verse 22). In heaven the saints are above the need of ordinances, which were the means of their preparation for heaven. When the end is attained, the means is no longer needed. Perfect and immediate communion with God will more than supply the place of gospel institutions.

2. The light in this city. Where there is no light, there can be no luster, no pleasure. Heaven is the inheritance of the saints in light. But what is that light? There is no sun or moon shining there. **The city does not need the sun or the moon to shine on it, for the glory of God gives it light, and the Lamb is its lamp** (verse 23). Light is sweet, and it is a pleasant thing to behold the sun. What is there in heaven that supplies this lack? There is no lack of the light of the sun, **for the glory of God gives it light, and the Lamb is its lamp.** God in Christ will be an everlasting fountain of knowledge and joy to the saints in heaven. And if this is so, there is no need for the sun or moon, any more than we need to light candles at noon when the sun is at full strength.

3. The inhabitants of the city. These are described in several ways:

a. By their number: whole nations of saved souls, some out of all nations, and many out of some nations. All those multitudes who were sealed on earth are saved in heaven.

b. By their dignity: some of the kings and princes of the earth, including some great kings. God will have some people from all ranks of men to fill the heavenly rooms—people of high rank and people of low rank. And when the greatest kings come to heaven, they will see all their former honor and glory swallowed up by this heavenly glory that so greatly exceeds it.

c. Their constant access and entry into this city. **On no day will its gates ever be shut, for there will be no night there** (verse 25). There is no night, and therefore there is no need to shut the gates. Someone or other is coming in every hour and moment. Those who are sanctified always find the gates open. They have an abundant entrance into the kingdom.

d. The accommodation of this city. **The glory and honor of the nations will be brought into it** (verse 26). Whatever is excellent and valuable in this world will be enjoyed in a greatly refined way and to a greater degree in heaven. There will be brighter crowns, made of a better and more enduring substance; there will be more enjoyable and satisfying feasts, a more glorious attendance, a truer sense of honor, and far higher posts of honor; a more glorious frame of mind, and a form and a countenance more glorious than was ever known in this world.

e. And lastly, the unpolluted purity of all who belong to the new Jerusalem. **Nothing impure will ever enter it, nor will anyone who does what is shameful or deceitful, but only those whose names are written in the Lamb's book of life** (verse 27).

(1) There the saints will have no impurity left in them. In death they will be cleansed from everything that defiles. On earth they feel a sad mixture of corruption with their graces, which hinders them in God's service, interrupts their communion with him, and intercepts the light of his countenance. But as they enter the Most Holy Place, they are washed in the bowl of Christ's blood and are presented to the Father spotless.

(2) There the saints will not have any impure person admitted with them. In the earthly Jerusalem a mixed communion is found, even after great care has been taken. Some roots of bitterness will sprout and cause trouble and defile Christian societies. But in the new Jerusalem there is a perfectly pure society.

First, it is free from people who are openly profane. No one who does abominable actions is allowed into heaven. In the churches on earth, abominable things are sometimes done, solemn ordinances are profaned and polluted in public for worldly ends. But such abominations have no place in heaven.

Second, it is free from hypocrites, such as liars and people pretending to be Jews but who are not. These kinds of people will creep into Christ's churches on earth and may lie there concealed for a long time, perhaps for their whole lives. But they cannot intrude into the new Jerusalem, which is wholly reserved for those who are called and chosen and who are faithful. It is only for those whose names are not only written in the register of the visible church, but **in the Lamb's book of life.**

Revelation
Chapter 22

Introduction

In this chapter we have:

1. A further description of the heavenly state of the church (verses 1-5).
2. A confirmation of this and all the other visions of this book (verses 6-19).
3. The conclusion (verses 20-21).

Verses 1-5

Then the angel showed me the river of the water of life, as clear as crystal, flowing from the throne of God and of the Lamb down the middle of the great street of the city. On each side of the river stood the tree of life, bearing twelve crops of fruit, yielding its fruit every month. And the leaves of the tree are for the healing of the nations. No longer will there be any curse. The throne of God and of the Lamb will be in the city, and his servants will serve him. They will see his face, and his name will be on their foreheads. There will be no more night. They will not need the light of a lamp or the light of the sun, for the Lord God will give them light. And they will reign for ever and ever.

The heavenly state that was previously described as a city and called the new Jerusalem is here described as a paradise. This alludes to the earthly paradise that was lost by the sin of the first Adam. Here is another paradise restored by the second Adam. A paradise in a city, or a whole city in a paradise! In the first paradise there were only two people to behold the beauty and taste its pleasures. But in this second paradise whole cities and nations will find abundant delight and satisfaction. Note here:

1. The river of paradise: **Then the angel showed me the river of the**

water of life, as clear as crystal, flowing from the throne of God and of the Lamb down the middle of the great street of the city (verses 1-2). The earthly paradise was well watered. No place can be pleasant or fruitful without water. This river is described:

a. By its fountainhead: **the throne of God and of the Lamb.** All our springs of grace, comfort, and glory are in God. And all our streams are from him, through the mediation of the Lamb.

b. By its quality: pure, **clear as crystal.** All the streams of earthly comfort are muddy. But these are clear, salutary, and refreshing, giving and preserving life to those who drink from it.

2. **The tree of life** in this paradise: On each side of the river stood the tree of life, bearing twelve crops of fruit, yielding its fruit every month. And the leaves of the tree are for the healing of the nations (verse 2). Such a tree was in the earthly paradise also. "And the LORD God made all kinds of trees grow out of the ground—trees that were pleasing to the eye and good for food. In the middle of the garden were the tree of life and the tree of the knowledge of good and evil" (Genesis 2:9). The tree of life in heaven far excels the tree of life on earth. As for this tree of life in heaven, note:

a. Where it is situated: **down the middle of the great street of the city. On each side of the river stood the tree of life** (verses 1-2). Or as we might have translated it, "in between the terrace and the river." This **tree of life** is fed by the pure waters of the river that comes from God's throne. The presence and perfections of God furnish all the glory and blessedness of heaven.

b. The fruitfulness of this tree.

(1) It bears many kinds of fruit, **bearing twelve crops** (verse 2), suited to the refined taste of all the saints.

(2) It bears fruit at all times: **yielding its fruit every month** (verse 2). This tree is never empty, never barren; there is always fruit on it. In heaven there is not only a variety of pure and satisfying pleasures, but a continuance of them, and always fresh.

(3) The fruit is not only pleasant but wholesome. The presence of God in heaven is the health and happiness of the saints. There they find in him a remedy for all their previous illnesses and are preserved by him in the most healthy and vigorous state.

c. The perfect freedom of this paradise from everything that is evil: **No longer will there be any curse. The throne of God and of the Lamb will be in the city, and his servants will serve him** (verse 3). **No longer will there be any curse.** There is no accursed being—no serpent, as there was in the earthly paradise. Here is the great excellency of this paradise—the devil has nothing to do there. He cannot distract the saints from serving God and make them subject to him, as he did with our first parents. Nor can the devil disturb the saints in God's service.

d. The supreme happiness of paradise.

(1) There the saints **will see [God's] face** (verse 4).What a beatific vision to enjoy!

(2) **They will see his face, and his name will be on their foreheads** (verse 4). God will own them, as they have his seal and name on their foreheads.

(3) **There will be no more night. They will not need the light of a lamp or the light of the sun, for the Lord God will give them light. And they will reign for ever and ever** (verse 5). **They will reign for ever and ever.** Their service will not only mean freedom but honor and dominion.

(4) All of this will be with perfect knowledge and joy. They will be full of wisdom and comfort, continually walking in the light of the Lord. This will not be just for a limited period of time, but **for ever and ever.**

Verses 6-19

The angel said to me, "These words are trustworthy and true. The Lord, the God of the spirits of the prophets, sent his angel to show his servants the things that must soon take place."

"Behold, I am coming soon! Blessed is he who keeps the words of the prophecy in this book."

I, John, am the one who heard and saw these things. And when I had heard and seen them, I fell down to worship at the feet of the angel who had been showing them to me. But he said to me, "Do not do it! I am a fellow servant with you and with your brothers the prophets and of all who keep the words of this book. Worship God!"

Then he told me, "Do not seal up the words of the prophecy of this book, because the time is near. Let him who does wrong continue to do wrong; let him who is vile continue to be vile; let him who does right continue to do right; and let him who is holy continue to be holy."

"Behold, I am coming soon! My reward is with me, and I will give to everyone according to what he has done. I am the Alpha and the Omega, the First and the Last, the Beginning and the End.

"Blessed are those who wash their robes, that they may have the right to the tree of life and may go through the gates into the city. Outside are the dogs, those who practice magic arts, the sexually immoral, the murderers, the idolaters and everyone who loves and practices falsehood.

"I, Jesus, have sent my angel to give you this testimony for the churches. I am the Root and the Offspring of David, and the bright Morning Star."

The Spirit and the bride say, "Come!" And let him who hears say, "Come!" Whoever is thirsty, let him come; and whoever wishes, let him take the free gift of the water of life.

I warn everyone who hears the words of the prophecy of this book:

If anyone adds anything to them, God will add to him the plagues described in this book. And if anyone takes words away from this book of prophecy, God will take away from him his share in the tree of life and in the holy city, which are described in this book.

We have here a solemn ratification of the contents of this book, and particularly of this last vision. But some people think it may refer not only to the whole book of Revelation, but to the whole New Testament, indeed to the whole Bible, completing and confirming the canon of Scripture.

1. This is confirmed by the name and nature of God who revealed these things: The angel said to me, "These words are trustworthy and true. The Lord, the God of the spirits of the prophets, sent his angel to show his servants the things that must soon take place" (verse 6). He is the Lord, and he is faithful and true, just as his words are trustworthy and true.

2. It is also confirmed by the messengers he chose to reveal these things to the world. The holy angels showed them to holy men of God. God would not use his angels and saints to deceive the world.

3. These words will soon be confirmed by their accomplishment. They are things that will shortly happen. Christ will make haste. "Behold, I am coming soon! Blessed is he who keeps the words of the prophecy in this book" (verse 7). "I am coming soon!" Then all doubts will be removed. Then those who have kept his words and believed him will prove to be the wise and happy people.

4. Confirmation is also given by the integrity of that angel who had been the apostle's guide and interpreter in these visions. That integrity was such that he not only refused to receive religious adoration from John but once again reproved him for it. I, John, am the one who heard and saw these things. And when I had heard and seen them, I fell down to worship at the feet of the angel who had been showing them to me. But he said to me, "Do not do it! I am a fellow servant with you and with your brothers the prophets and of all who keep the words of this book. Worship God!" (verses 8-9). He who was so tender about God's honor and so displeased with what was wrong toward God would never come in God's name to lead God's people into mere dreams and delusions. It is yet another confirmation about the apostle's sincerity that he confesses his own sin and the folly into which he had again lapsed. He leaves a lasting record of his failing. This shows that he was a faithful and impartial writer.

5. This book is confirmed by the order given to leave the book of the prophecy open, to be perused by all, so that they might labor to understand it, that they might make their objections about it and compare the prophecy with the events. Then he told me, "Do not seal up the words of the prophecy of this book, because the time is near" (verse 10). God deals here freely and openly with everyone. He does not speak in secret but calls everyone to bear witness to the declarations made.

6. It is confirmed by the effect that this book, thus kept open, will have

on people: "Let him who does wrong continue to do wrong; let him who is vile continue to be vile; let him who does right continue to do right; and let him who is holy continue to be holy" (verse 11). Those who are unclean and unjust will take that opportunity to be more unclean and more unjust. But it will confirm, strengthen, and further sanctify those who are upright with God. It will be a savor of life to some, and of death to others, and so will be seen to be from God. "Behold, I am coming soon! My reward is with me, and I will give to everyone according to what he has done" (verse 12).

7. It will be Christ's rule of judgment at the great day. He will give rewards and punishment to people depending on how their deeds agree or disagree with God's Word. Therefore, that Word itself has to be true and faithful.

8. "I am the Alpha and the Omega, the First and the Last, the Beginning and the End" (verse 13). This is the word of him who is the author, finisher, and rewarder of the faith and holiness of his people. He is the First and the Last, the same from first to last, and so is his Word. "Blessed are those who wash their robes, that they may have the right to the tree of life and may go through the gates into the city" (verse 14). He will by his Word give to his people who conform themselves to it the right to the tree of life—that is, entry into heaven. This will be full confirmation of the truth and authority of his Word, since it contains the title and evidence of that confirmed state of holiness and happiness that remains for the people of heaven.

9. It is a book that condemns and excludes from heaven all wicked, unrighteous people. "Outside are the dogs, those who practice magic arts, the sexually immoral, the murderers, the idolaters and everyone who loves and practices falsehood" (verse 15). In particular it excludes "everyone who loves and practices falsehood." Therefore, this book can never itself be a lie.

10. This book is confirmed by the testimony of Jesus, who is the Spirit of prophecy. "I, Jesus, have sent my angel to give you this testimony for the churches. I am the Root and the Offspring of David, and the bright Morning Star" (verse 16). This Jesus, as God, is the Root . . . of David, though as man he is the Offspring of David. He is a person in whom all uncreated and created excellencies meet. He is too great and too good to deceive his churches in the world. He is the fountain of all light, the bright Morning Star, and as such has given to his churches this morning light of prophecy, to assure them of the light of that perfect day that is approaching.

11. It is confirmed by an open and general invitation to everyone to come and take part in the promises and privilege of the Gospel, those streams of living water. The Spirit and the bride say, "Come!" And let him who hears say, "Come!" Whoever is thirsty, let him come; and whoever wishes, let him take the free gift of the water of life (verse 17).

These are offered to all who have in their souls a thirst that this world cannot quench.

12. It is confirmed by the combined testimony of the Spirit of God and that gracious spirit that is in all the true members of God's church. **The Spirit and the bride** join in testifying about the truth and excellence of the Gospel.

13. Lastly, it is confirmed by a most solemn sanction. **I warn everyone who hears the words of the prophecy of this book: If anyone adds anything to them, God will add to him the plagues described in this book. And if anyone takes words away from this book of prophecy, God will take away from him his share in the tree of life and in the holy city, which are described in this book** (verses 18-19). Everyone who dares to corrupt or change God's Word, by adding to it or taking away from it, is condemned and cursed. He who adds to the Word of God adds to himself **the plagues described in this book.** And he who takes anything away from this book cuts himself off from all its promises and privileges.

This sanction is like a flaming sword that guards the canon of Holy Scripture from profane hands. God surrounds his law with the fence, "Do not add to what I command you and do not subtract from it, but keep the commands of the LORD your God that I give you" (Deuteronomy 4:2), and also the whole Old Testament ("Remember the law of my servant Moses, the decrees and laws I gave him at Horeb for all Israel," Malachi 4:4), and now, in the most solemn manner, the whole Bible. This assures us that this book has a most sacred nature, with divine authority, and therefore the special care of the great God.

Verses 20-21

He who testifies to these things says, "Yes, I am coming soon."
Amen. Come, Lord Jesus.
The grace of the Lord Jesus be with God's people. Amen.

We now come to the conclusion of the whole book. This comes in three parts:

1. Christ's farewell to his church. He seems now, after he had been revealing these things to his people on earth, to take leave of them and return to heaven. But he leaves them with great kindness and assures them that it will not be long before he comes again. **He who testifies to these things says, "Yes, I am coming soon." Amen. Come, Lord Jesus** (verse 20). **"Yes, I am coming soon."** Just as when he ascended into heaven after his resurrection he left a promise about his gracious presence, so here he parts with a promise about his speedy return. Some might say, "Where is the promise of his return being fulfilled, when so many ages have gone by since this was written?" Let such people know that God is not slack about keeping the promises he has made to his people, but is long-suffering

toward his enemies. His coming will be sooner than they realize, sooner than they are prepared for, sooner than they desire. But to his people it will be at the right season. The vision is about an appointed time, and he will not delay. **"Yes, I am coming soon."** Let this word always be echoing in our ear, and let us be diligent to be found in a state of peace with and in him, spotless and with no defect.

2. The church's heartfelt echo to Christ's promise.

a. Declaring her firm belief in it. **Amen.** "So it is, so it will be."

b. Expressing her earnest desire for it. **Come, Lord Jesus.** "Even so, come Lord Jesus; come quickly, my Beloved." "Come away, my lover, and be like a gazelle or like a young stag on the spice-laden mountains" (Song of Songs 8:14). Thus beats the pulse of the church; thus breathes the gracious Spirit that actuates and informs the mystical body of Christ. We should never be satisfied until we find such a spirit breathing in us, making us look for the blessed hope and glorious appearing of the great God and our Saviour Jesus Christ. This is the language of the church of the firstborn, and we should join other believers in this song, often reminding ourselves of his promise. What comes from heaven in a promise should be sent back to heaven in a prayer. **Come, Lord Jesus** ends this state of sin, sorrow, and temptation. "Gather your people out of this present evil world and take them up to heaven, that state of perfect purity, peace, and joy, and so finish your great purpose and fulfill all your words in which your people have put their hope."

3. The apostolic blessing that concludes the whole book: **The grace of the Lord Jesus be with God's people. Amen** (verse 21). Note here:

a. The Bible ends with clear evidence about the Godhead of Christ, since the Spirit of God teaches the apostle to bless his people in the name of Christ, and to ask Christ for a blessing on them. This is a proper act of adoration.

b. We should desire nothing more than that Christ's grace should be with us in this world, to prepare us for the glory of Christ in the other world. It is by his grace that we must be kept in a joyful expectation of his glory and become fit for this and persevere in it. His glorious appearing will be joyful and welcome for those who take part in his grace and favor here. Therefore, to this most comprehensive prayer we should all add our heartfelt **Amen.** We should most earnestly thirst after greater measures of the gracious influences of the blessed Jesus in our souls and his gracious presence with us, for he is our Sun and Shield. "For the LORD God is a sun and a shield; the LORD bestows favor and honor; no good thing does he withhold from those whose walk is blameless" (Psalm 84:11).